Turning Points

Jim Smoke

D0596623

HARVEST HOUSE PUBLISHERS
Eugene, Oregon 97402

Other books by Jim Smoke:

Growing Through Divorce
Living Beyond Divorce
Suddenly Single
Every Single Day

Videocassette series: *How To Survive a Divorce*

TURNING POINTS

Acknowledgements

Special thanks to Robert Hawkins, Sr., publisher and friend, who first suggested I write a book called *Growing Through Divorce* in 1975.

To my manuscript typist and friend Diana White.

To all the people I know who have helped me navigate the many turning points I have come to in my journey through life.

Contents

Introduction

I have always been intrigued with the question "What brings people to turning points in their lives?" Are they situations that simply explode on you when you least expect them, or are they preplanned events that can be carefully orchestrated?

Turning Points is a journey of exploration into the things that cause us to come to turning points, identify them when they appear, and successfully handle them as we wind our way through life.

The Bible gives strong and clear directions for each of us as we look closely at our turning points. It becomes our road map for exploring the question "Where to from here, God?"

Journey with us as we explore the things great and small that send us off in new directions in our lives.

Jim Smoke
Orange, California
1985

1

Proceed With Caution! Life Under Construction!

1

Proceed With Caution!
Life Under Construction!

Do you have a street or highway in your town that always seems to be in a state of repair? About the only progress that the repair crews seem to make is to place the warning signs in different locations! As you wind your way through the construction tangle day after day, you begin to wonder if the repair process will ever be completed. You eventually lose patience with the process and look for an alternate route to your destination.

Your life and my life is a lot like a roadway under repair. At times we are challenged and excited about the end results. At other times we are frustrated and impatient that the process seems to take so long. The real difficulty is that we are both the repair crew and the person passing through the obstructions. Our greatest danger is that we will try to find someone to do our repair work for us while we sit on the sidelines and offer our criticisms at the slowness of the process.

There will be times in each of our lives when we are under construction. Sometimes the construction will be of the minor variety and not interrupt our journey very much. At other times it will be of major proportion and cause our lives to slow down, contemplate detours, plan new routes, and move off in new directions. In effect, we will look back on these times as significant turning points in our lives. My concern in this book is that we learn to identify our turning points and to deal with their effect on our lives. Another concern is to be able to look back at them when we work through them and allow them to give us strong motivation for facing the ones still ahead of us.

One of the things I am amazed at in the Scriptures is the way the Old Testament leaders constantly reminded Israel of what God had done for them in the yesterdays of their lives. Each time they faced new turning points, the strong road signs of yesterday's victories through God's power gave them hope for their journey into today. It enabled them (and us) to know that God is still in the construction business.

One of the things I am discovering as I grow older is that my personal turning points from yesterday are more easily identifiable today. That's no great mystery, because our hindsight is always 20-20. Our great struggle is for clear foresight. However, I need to know where I have been if I am to know where I am going. I want to be able to identify my own turning points, what brought me to them, and how I responded to them.

In 1970 we moved from Florida to California. If someone would have offered me a script of what the next 15 years in California held for me and my family as we flew West, I am certain I would have asked the pilot to turn around and let me stay forever on the white, sandy beaches of Florida! To those of you who are always wanting to know what is ahead, let me suggest that some days you will not want to know until you arrive there. Leaving the South for the West was a major turning point in all our lives. The 15 years since then have contained joys and sorrows, victories and tragedies, peaks and valleys. Our greatest danger when looking back is to remember only the problems we have experienced in turning a new direction in our lives. Problems and struggles always seem to loom larger in memory than joys and happiness. When Israel got tired of eating manna day after day in the wilderness, they began complaining and thinking back to the joys of eating the leeks and garlic of Egypt. They somehow forgot the slavery attached to their Egyptian diet. They also forgot that manna and freedom went together!

This year we find ourselves at another major turning point in our lives. It's one that every parent faces in the child-rearing process. It's known as the empty-nest syndrome. Everyone seems to have a different response to it. Many of my friends have listened to their teenagers telling them that they just can't wait to be out of the house and on their own. And many of us as parents have said "Go for it!" under our breath. But when the actual time arrives for the big move out in our own family, we find ourselves wanting our children to both go and stay. We know that things will never again be as they once were and we are not sure of what is yet to come. It is a turning point! We want it and we don't want it. We somehow want a guarantee that this juncture in the road of life will be smooth and well-managed.

I recently observed a turning point in an older relative. This person had reached the "give everything away" state of life. Looking at the short end of the journey, there was no apparent need to keep acquiring things now in this individual's journey. It appeared to be a time to lighten the load of acquisitions. I thought of the process that we all seem to go through in life. In our young years we are constantly adding to life's baggage by buying everything we can. When we were first married, everything we owned could be moved across the state in a U-Haul trailer. After three children, it took one of Bekins' best to move us across the country! We were on the journey of possession. Now, in midlife, we are starting to sort out what we really don't need any longer. We are also discovering that people matter more than things! Getting things is a turning point. Giving things away is another turning point. Most of us would have made poor pioneers in early America. Our possessions would never have fit into a covered wagon!

I remembered when our first child arrived. The day we brought him home from the hospital, we lost the freedom to come and go as we pleased. We also lost the freedom of an undisturbed night of sleeping for quite some time. We had to think for three people rather than two. Babysitters became part of our lifestyle. It even changed our method of transportation. Our sports car just did not have the "baby baggage" capacity we now needed. The baby changed our eating habits from "food goes on the inside" to "food goes all over the outside"! People had warned us that our lives would change, but we disregarded their threats. It was a big turning point for us.

We are brought to turning points in our lives by both planned and unplanned events. The planned are usually the easiest to handle: They are predictable. Other people have been there before us and can give us advice. We can learn from their mistakes. They can cheer for us, support us, and tell us that we will survive. They can even write books for us about their adventures. Planned events have histories; unplanned ones are mysteries—they tend to leave us confused, anxious, and fearful. We feel out of control.

I planned to go to college to receive some sort of an education. I did not plan to go into the ministry as a result of my college years. The two unplanned events that led me into ministry were spending a summer traveling and speaking on a college gospel team and being invited to speak every Sunday at a small Methodist church that could not afford a pastor. These two things were not a part of my planned event of college. Yet these two things, plus a few others along the way, led me into 26 years of ministry. I just wanted to go to college and get smarter!

Marrying my wife was not a planned event. I just wanted to have a date with her and take her ice skating. That was the plan, and I had no plans beyond that plan. In case you might misunderstand, after many dates and many months we did plan to get married, but when we first dated that was not part of my plan.

As I look back on my life, I realize that many of my turning points came from the unplanned event rather than the planned. And I take pride in the fact that I am a planner and well-organized most of the time. I seldom leave things to chance or happenstance. Perhaps good planning is allowing for the unplanned to enter your life and allowing you to move in a previously unplanned direction.

Unplanned events in most of our lives are looked upon as deadly intruders of our peace of mind. They are seldom welcomed and mostly feared. They get in the way of where we are going. Our immediate response is to remove them or avoid them or spend a great deal of time asking the question "Why me?" It is so difficult to inject Romans 8:28 into an unplanned event. We want an instant answer to the "Why?" instead of a process answer that takes time in coming. Romans 8:28 states, "We know that all things work together for good." Some of the unplanned events that bring us to turning points are not pleasant to experience. In fact many of them are just plain rotten. In a later chapter we will talk about turning points through crisis experiences. Most people do not celebrate a crisis by throwing a party. They often suffer silently through their crisis, hoping that the pain will eventually be replaced by healing and growth.

Unplanned events in the lives of other people can bring us to turning points in our own lives. Sickness and death are two of the most common unplanned events in the lives of those around us that can have a bearing on the future direction of our own life. Divorce, a largely unthought-of and unplanned-for event in the lives of well over a million Americans every year, can drastically affect the lives of children, in-laws, families, social networks, and communities.

Some time ago a person asked me which five people had been the greatest influence for growth upon my life. I had never been asked that in a direct way before, and I have spent some time since then thinking about it. At different ages and different times, my life has been molded in special ways by special people. None of them were a prominently planned part of the landscape of my life. They were not even in the mainstream of my existence. Yet their contributions to my life over the years have enabled me to negotiate significant turning points. They have been affirmers and encouragers, prodders and catalysts for my journey. They have been part of my ongoing construction crew. Who are the people who fit that description in your life? How long has it been since you checked your life? Who are the new ones that are banging on the door of your life to make further contributions?

Ten years of traveling across this country has brought me into community with many new friends. I did not plan to meet any of them ten years ago. Yet they have become part of the come-and-go structure of my life and have helped me through intersections and busy thoroughfares in my life. I could refer to them as the "unplanned people." Yet I believe they were planned by God to be His friendly interruptions in my life.

Unplanned people in your life come with different messages for you. Sometimes you will find yourself not wanting to hear the messenger or the message. Pride keeps the messenger at a safe distance. Ego says, "Who are they to tell me?"

God specialized in using messengers in both the Old and New Testaments. One of His better messengers is found in the person of a "nobody special" named Jahaziel in 2 Chronicles chapter 20. In the midst of a tense situation, God spoke directly through Jahaziel to King Jehoshaphat and all Israel with the message to "not be afraid nor dismayed because of this great multitude, for the battle is not yours, but God's" (2 Chronicles 20:15). God could have spoken through the king himself, but He chose one of His unplanned people to get His word across.

Most of us would like God's messenger to us to come in the person of a Billy Graham or some other well-known Christian leader. They would get our attention immediately and be far more believable. But that's not how God works with you and me most of the time. We may miss many messages because we are unwilling to receive the messenger.

I have an inordinate attraction to stories of people who for years have done one thing in career or vocation and all of a sudden stop doing that thing to do something brand new. I recently read about a New York advertising man who left his career at the height of success, took his family, and moved to the wilds of Alaska to start a whole new life and career as a trapper. I want to cheer for a somebody who got unstuck and gave up a planned lifestyle for an unplanned one. At certain moments of my day, I want to go and join him in his new adventure. Many of us would follow him in our mind and spirit if not in our hired moving van. We have a secret admiration for his spunk, daring, and casting of caution to the winds. Gail Sheehy in her book *Pathfinders* tells the stories of many people who took adventures similar to our friend from New York.

We finally live in an age when one can take the great leap to a new lifestyle at any point in his or her journey. Most of us grew up with the planned lifestyle that scripted us for education, profession, career, marriage, and suburbs, in that order. We tied a caboose called retirement to the end of the list, and our whole train was ready to roll. But someplace along the tracks of life our train seems to stall, and we realize that we don't want to continue doing what we have been doing so far. Our planned lifestyle needs a turning point.

When people that I do not know pick me up at airports, I usually try to start a conversation by asking them what they do. When they answer, I ask them *why* they do that. I receive funny looks and funnier answers to that question— comments like ''That's what I was trained to do'' or ''That's what I have always done'' or ''That's what our family has always done'' or sometimes ''That's what everyone said I would be good at.'' If I am brave, I ask how long they have lived in the town we are in. I follow that by asking why they live there. I seem to get the same set of answers as I did to the first question. Now I confess to you that I don't travel around America to get people upset at what they do and where they live. I guess I am just intrigued by their responses and wonder if they are simply living out a planned lifestyle without ever questioning why.

You are probably thinking that a planned, ordered lifestyle is the best and most comfortable way to live. And I want you to know that I am all in favor of order and comfort. I am also nervous about ruts, cocoons, sameness, and boredom. They seem to be easy places for you and me to go to sleep and never hear what's going on around us. Most of us would rather live in the comfort zone than the combat zone.

As I study the Scriptures, I am acutely aware that God was the disturber of people suffering with the cocoon complex. He had a way of shattering the cocoon and launching the person into a whole new lifestyle. The disciples in the Gospels are perhaps the best aggregate example of this. They were called from their planned lifestyle, events, and friendships to follow Jesus and become "fishers of men." It probably sounded adventuresome to them, even though they had little understanding of the experience yet to come for each of them. Perhaps it sounded just enough better than what they were locked into for them to say, "Why not?"

Although the Scripture doesn't record it, I can just imagine what happened when they got around to their old friends to tell them about their change in lifestyle. I am not sure how they even described their new vocation and calling to others. It certainly might have sounded like they all went from employment to unemployment. I can just see all their friends shaking their heads and wondering if they had been out in the sun too long. Their new leader, Jesus, was looked upon with skepticism and disbelief by most of their community. Yet there was an adventure looming out of the invitation to "follow and become." Their turning point came when they said, "I want to do that!"

A change in lifestyle is often an invitation to uncertainty.

Because we live in an age of the certain, the uncertain looks dangerous and threatening. It holds out no guarantees to us. It offers grand and glorious insecurity in a world that sells insurance for everything.

Abraham had it all together—his lifestyle, his wealth, his family, his flocks, his lands, his world. It was God who became his disturber and called him to a new journey, a new land, and a new promise. The promise could not have been fulfilled if he had said, "Lord, do it, but let me stay here and enjoy it my way." God was the shaker of Abraham's lifestyle, along with that of his offspring throughout the Scriptures. Abraham gained by giving up a lifestyle he had known for one that was unknown. He would probably concur with the words of the late missionary Jim Elliott, who said in 1949 while still in college, "He is no fool who gives what he cannot keep to gain what he cannot lose."

There is probably no stronger word in our culture today than *lifestyle*. It describes everything, anything, and nothing about the way we all live. It is as varied as the people who live it out. It changes overnight. We are in pursuit of it with everything we have at our disposal. And all those just one step above us seem to have it! You and I are trying to make that next step so that we can have it also.

Being under construction means being open to the unplanned events, people, and lifestyles that God has for us just around the next corner. It means that our eyes are open to His turning points for us. It means that we are not moving so rapidly that we are missing the signposts He has erected along our roadways.

My wife and I have gotten into our regular summer habit of taking evening walks around our neighborhood. I am always amazed at how much more you can see when on foot than when whizzing down the streets in your car. We stop at the various flower gardens and attempt to smell the roses. It is hard to smell the roses at 30 miles per hour. It is hard to even *see* the roses at 30 miles per hour! It is also hard to talk to the neighbors at 30 miles per hour!

Turning points in my life seem to come when I least expect them. We have already said that much of the time they are unplanned. That's why they are so easy to miss. I am well aware that God has the ability to clobber us sometimes to draw our attention to a turning point. Occasionally He does that for you and me. However, I feel that a great deal of the time He wants you and me to be sufficiently perceptive and in tune with Him to get the message without the divine muscle.

Another thought that deals with being under construction and open to turning points centers in unplanned renewal. The Scriptures talk in numerous places about the process of renewal. We sing old and new hymns that encourage us toward renewal. We plan churchwide renewal conferences, and when they are over we often go back to business as usual...nonrenewed! We all crave to be touched by renewal, and yet we avoid it like the plague. Our fear of it seems to be centered in our inability to control it once it happens to us. Renewal has an unpredictable quality about it that makes us nervous. Yet we long for it, dream of it, seek to program it, and go thirsty because of a lack of it.

I believe that renewal is largely an unplanned event. By trying to plan it, we eliminate it from happening. It has to happen from the inside out in you and me, not from the outside in. It comes from the deep inner stirring of God's Spirit down inside each of us. I remember the words of the old song we sang in my church when I was growing up: "Send a great revival; start the work in *me!*" That's a nervous prayer to pray. I am not sure of the understanding we have of the implications of "in *me.*" It involves our willingness to put out the UNDER CONSTRUCTION sign and know that we are at a turning point in our life and growth.

The Israelites lived a yo-yo existence much of the time. When they were living right and God was blessing them, they were on top. When they were living wrong and there was no blessing, they were on the bottom. Prophets, priests, and kings sought the blessing of renewal from God for Israel when they were on the bottom. The theme of renewal and refreshing is a recurring one throughout the Old Testament. It is evident in Paul's teachings to the early church. It jumps out at us today in the dry and barren places of our faith. We sing about showers of blessings but are afraid to get wet!

Renewal starts with the inside journey for each of us. It is being in pursuit of what God has for us and being open to it as He reveals it to us. For me, it is more process than earthshaking revelation. It is being open to hear the Scripture that says, "Be still and know that I am God."

Are you willing to put your UNDER CONSTRUCTION signs out for all to see? Are you willing to put them out for God to see? If you are, there will be some turning points in this book for your life.

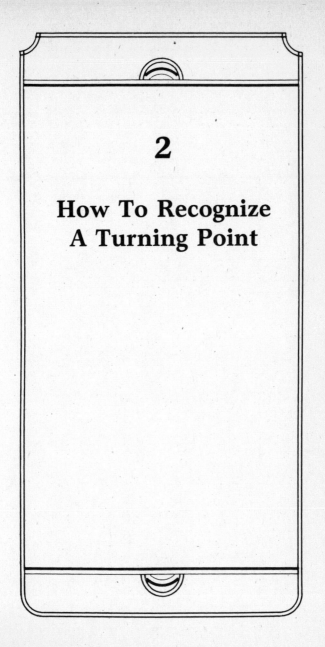

2

How To Recognize
A Turning Point

2

How To Recognize
A Turning Point

Most people can look back over the years and
identify a time and place at which their lives
changed significantly. Whether by accident or
design, these are the moments, when because of
a readiness within us, we are forced to seriously
reappraise ourselves and the conditions under
which we live and to make certain choices that
will affect the rest of our lives.
—Frederic F. Flach, M.D., in *Choices*

Dealing with a turning point in your life is only half the
battle. The rest of it centers on learning how to recognize
turning points when they appear on the landscape of your
life. I have discovered that turning points don't always come
in attractively wrapped packages. They seldom come
attached to giant STOP signs. They have a way of sneaking
up on you and clobbering you when you aren't looking.
Sometimes they touch you very gently, and if you are not
sensitive you will miss the signal. You seldom get an
announcement over a loudspeaker proclaiming that this or
that is a turning point!

In the above quote, Dr. Flach talks about a "readiness within" that allows us to recognize a need for a change or a turning point. Events, experiences, and situations all have a way of preparing us on the inside for things to happen on the outside.

When we plant a garden, we prepare the soil before we plant the flowers. Then we tend the soil and the flowers after planting. Preparation and care form the key to a beautiful garden. The same principle is true as you and I move in new directions for our lives. Inner readiness for change is a greater priority than external readiness. If the inner man cannot meet the challenge of the outer experience, the turning point can turn into a merry-go-round ride. The great tendency in our society is to deal with the external first; it gives quicker visual results. The internal is quiet and often goes virtually unnoticed for a long period of time.

Some Internal Homework Questions

There are several questions that I have shared with people individually as they struggle with the internal recognition of a turning point. These questions take time to think through and evaluate. They are not simple YES or NO questions. I would suggest that you both think and write your responses to them. They are inclusive and can be applied to any and every area of your life in regard to change.

1. *Why am I doing what I am doing? What is the real reason for it, and does that reason justify the continual process?* Some people do all the wrong things for all the right reasons. Others do all the right things for all the wrong reasons. Still others have no reason for anything they do. Many people do things for outward reward and public affirmation. Human applause is both the motivator and the rewarder. A warm spirit of inner satisfaction is often traded for whatever will bring the quickest outward payoff.

Our society can often be broken down into two groups

of people: those who work for monetary gain as a sole reward for their labors and those who want to work with and for people to help them through life's struggles.

The "Why am I doing what I am doing?" question applies to vocation, relationships, daily behavior patterns, goals, thoughts, feelings, life situations, religious faith and community . . . every area of your life.

When do most people wrestle with this kind of question? Usually when everything they are doing starts to go wrong. If you wait this long, the danger is that you will look for Band-Aid solutions rather than long-term changes. In counseling many people through divorce, I am always asked the same question: "How long will it take to get rid of my pain, and what can I do about it?"

My response is that there is no growth without pain, and it usually takes about two to three years. And I listen to the groans!

How much better for you and me to review our lives when the pressure is not on us and things are not falling apart! I believe that everyone should take a long weekend once or twice a year for a *life review* time. No radios, TV's, entertainment, etc. Just you alone and a pad on which to write your feelings, thoughts, and observations. A good place to do this is at some kind of retreat setting. Here you can be in a spiritual atmosphere and yet have the peace and solitude you need for thinking, writing, and praying. Most of us think of a retreat as a time to be with many other people at a camp or conference center (and we need that too), but we also need to order a "retreat for one, please" once in a while.

Many of us are pressured into doing things because that is what other people think we ought to do. Early in life we start collecting the opinions of others. The problem is that we quit collecting them and start living them out in our later years. We then move from collecting and living to blaming. Wasn't it Adam who started playing the blame game first when he said, "The woman whom You gave to be with me, she gave me of the tree, and I ate" (Genesis 3:12)? What do you think I should do? I'll do it! It's your fault because you made me do it!

Answer the first question honestly. It can be a major turning point for you.

2. *Is what I am doing the BEST use of my gifts, talents, and abilities?* Most of us function best and are happiest when we are employing the things we are most gifted in. This does not mean that you are doing what is easiest. It means that you are doing what is most natural to you. I always admire people who can fix things. I don't fix anything because my best talent does not lie in that area. I either call a repairman (a few of them should be doing other things also!) or my wife, who can fix anything. It used to bother me, but I have finally accepted the fact that I am not talented in that area. Give me an audience to speak to and a book to write, and I think I am in the right ballpark.

You are probably wondering how you discover your gifts and talents. I think this is a process that never ends. You most certainly don't do it all before you are 25. Both Grandma Moses and Colonel Sanders didn't get going until they were in the retirement-age group. Some of us need to have our gifts called forth by those around us. Our youngest daughter did not know she had any art ability until an art teacher discovered her talent when she signed up for an "easy" class in her junior year in high school. That teacher was observant enough to see the gift and call it forth. Today that daughter is pursuing a career in fashion design. I cringe to think what would have happened if that teacher would have looked at her first assignment and told her to take some other class.

I meet many people who are plugged into the wrong outlet and experience extreme unhappiness because of it. If you are not in a place where you are getting the best mileage out of what you have, and the promise of that is not on your horizon, you may be at a turning point in your life.

What are your gifts? Are you using them in every area of your life? Here again, we are not just referring to vocational areas but to all the areas we listed in the first question.

There are laypeople working and serving in church ministries who should be doing something else because they simply are not gifted for what they are doing. They are often dragged into a job because they are told there is no one else to do it and are made to feel guilty if they don't do it.

Spiritual gifts have a great deal to do with this area. There are many good books on the subject at your Christian bookstore, so we will not go into that here.

3. *Does what I do in the many areas of my life cause me more happiness than unhappiness?* The sign in the restaurant window said "TGIF!" By translation it meant "Thank God It's Friday!" Why? Because it meant the end of the workweek and a release from the nine-to-five job of the past five days. As people hoist their own TGIF flags at the end of each working week, I wonder how many can look back and say that they received more happiness than unhappiness in their 40-hour pursuit of making a living.

Do your friends and support systems cause you more happiness than unhappiness? I am amazed at how many people continue and maintain relationships with other people that cause them a high level of misery. I am aware that you cannot just junk every unpleasant relationship that you have in life. But you can review them and either seek to change them or depart from them.

Toxic relationships kill your spirit and affect the attitudes you have toward other people. As you carry happiness, you can also carry poison. Some people live in marriages that have long since died. They continue to serve a sentence called marriage but have abandoned all efforts to rekindle the once-alive spark in their loving relationship. Due to their unhappiness, they give constant injections of poison to each other and to those in their support systems.

What's happening to you right now in your happiness

levels? Are you at a turning point and willing to take an honest look at your situation? Can you pinpoint the unhappiness? Can you make some decisions to deal with that unhappiness and send your life in a new direction?

4. *Am I free to live with the I CAN rather than the I SHOULD?* Many of us daily fall victim to the *I should*'s of life. We carry around a long list of our *should do*'s. I have discovered that some of mine are healthy but that many more are unhealthy and simply provoke a giant guilt complex in me when I am unable to carry them out. *Can do* gives me a choice. *Should do* gives me a complex. I am aware that there is always a fine line between the two, and I have to be able to discern where that line is. *Should*'s usually cause a mental pileup in our minds that can easily lead to stomach upset and ulcerous conditions. We can easily fall victim to the tyranny and control of our *should do* list. The *should*'s are things we look back over our shoulder at. The *can*'s are things we look forward to with excitement and expectation. If you were to sit down right now and write out two long lists in both of these areas, which of the two would be the longer and more controlling in your life? Reaching a turning point is deciding by an act of the will that you will no longer allow yourself to be controlled and dominated by a list of things that can never be ultimately fulfilled.

Often those around us give us our life of *should do*'s. Because we are not in charge of ourselves, we tell them they are right and allow their lists to be injected into our daily routine. *I should* put my garbage out tonight because it's Tuesday and the garbage collectors come tomorrow morning. *I can* or *I cannot* put it out. It is my choice, but if I don't do it, it will simply pile up for another week and I will face the same choice next Tuesday evening. Happiness is turning your *should do*'s into *can do*'s.

The Finality of Turning Points

One of the reasons many people avoid turning points

centers in their fear of making an irreversible decision. Good logic and wisdom tells me that a turning point can also be viewed as a testing point or trial point. If this sounds like an escape hatch to you, I don't mean it to be. I do want to show that a turning point will not always be set in cement but will allow you a place to test a new way in your life.

Most of us who have raised a child or two have gone through the experience of music lessons. Sometimes the ordeal is initiated by the parent, sometimes by the sincere desire of the child to learn a new thing. When most children discover that they will not master the instrument of their choosing in 18 months, they often grow weary with practice and want to quit altogether. After a few parent battles and statements like "You started this and I'm paying for it and you're going to finish it!" we surrender and the child quits the lessons. Only a few months later that same child can come up to you and ask if she can take ballet classes. What's your response? "No! You never finished your piano lessons!" Based on the incompleted first experience, the second is denied.

I have learned something over the years about this kind of thing: You have the freedom to start and the freedom to stop and the freedom to start something entirely new, and this does not mean that you have failed at one or the other. Who made the law that said once a direction is chosen, one cannot deviate from it? Some adults I know are still living out the lesson format that their parents established for them years ago. They almost need permission to stop something and take off in a new direction.

A turning point can be a test of the new. It can be a challenge for new growth. But it should never be a sentence for the future.

Fear often plays an important part in our turning points. I confess to you that I always have a fear when I start a new book. I fear that it will not be as good as the first one or the last one. I fear that no one will buy it. (That's called economic fear!) I fear that what I write will not be helpful to anyone or at least not to as many people as I had hoped. I fear I will run out of gas halfway through the project. I fear that no publisher will ask me to write another book after this one. Those are pretty real fears that follow hard on the heels of writing the first page for this book. Your list is probably like mine. It is relative to your own turning point.

One of the things that has helped me a great deal is understanding that I have the freedom to fail. Put another way, I have the freedom to not be locked in by things that do not turn out as I have planned them. I believe that most of us have an abiding fear of failure that usually looms largest in our life when we decide to make a new decision and head in a new direction. We are hounded by the "what if?" nagging at our spirits.

One of the greatest lessons I have learned from Scripture is that a Christian has the freedom to fail and yet not be considered by God to *be* a failure. I read the scriptural accounts of Peter and see his life intertwined with both success and failure. Even after he denied Christ, he eventually rebounded from the shadows to the sunlight. Jesus did not put him out to pasture due to his failure. Failure, if it is anything, is a learning experience. If this were not true, none of us would be walking today. We would all still be crawling across living room floors, office floors, and through life. The first time we tried to walk, we probably fell. But this did not deter us, nor those who were attempting to introduce us to a new kind of mobility. We all failed walking at least once. But we kept on trying.

It is very difficult to find any biblical heroes who did not allow their humanity to get in the way of their journey for God. Many even went in the wrong direction and had to correct their course down the road. We will explore this more in later chapters.

A turning point is not a sentence. It is an opportunity to introduce change into your life. There is no need to view it as a last recourse or your final shot at doing something right or different in life. A turning point is letting go of one thing and attaching to another. It is extremely difficult, if not impossible, to try to add new things without letting go of any of the old things. There is always an element of risk involved with a new discovery of trust. We will talk about both of these later.

Our choices which lead to turning points are life-affecting to us personally and to those around us. I don't believe we should treat them lightly. We need to do our homework, to allow time for processing, and to weigh the long-term gains against the short-time excitement. Exploring and facing turning points is not a filler for idle moments. It is life-construction work!

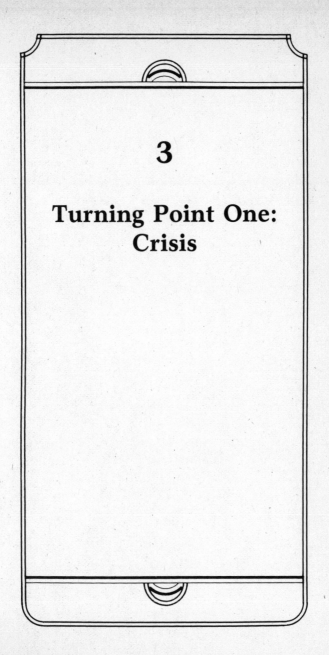

3

Turning Point One:
Crisis

3

Turning Point One: Crisis

The changing of the seasons is like the turning-point times in human life. Like the seasons of the earth, that seem to challenge and threaten life, the crisis times of human life are rich sources of ever-present and dangerous opportunities for new life. . . . Like the result of the falling and decay of leaves that is revealed only in the richness of soil that gives new life in spring, so the resurrection time of human life becomes apparent only after we have walked through the darkness of an ending to a new beginning.
—Paula Ripple in *Called to Be Friends*

Have you ever met the kind of people who seem to be constantly living in a state of crisis? If they can't find a real crisis to be involved in, they invent one. They seem to thrive on crisis experiences. They live in a daily state of churning emotions. They don't work for resolution and settlement. They seem to thrive on agitation created by crisis.

There is another kind of people that we all know. Instead of looking for a crisis to happen, they run as fast and as far

as they can from any hint that they will have to experience
a crisis. If the crisis catches up with them, they stick their
head in the sand until it passes or someone else resolves it.

Most of us find ourselves somewhere between these two
extremes. We admit that a crisis now and then adds some
challenge and excitement to our lives, but we don't want
anything of any major proportion. Minor crises make good
table talk; major ones scare us.

Living in Southern California means living with the omi-
nous threat of the Great Earthquake. Periodic television programs attempt to warn us of the impending event and equip
us with the knowledge of how to survive it when it happens. Hardly anyone here spends any amount of time thinking about this kind of crisis and how he or she would survive
it. Few have taken out earthquake insurance. When we lived
in Florida, the threat was hurricanes. When we lived in the
Midwest, it was tornadoes. It would appear that there is an
imminent weather crisis just waiting to happen in any part
of America. Yet we do not live in a constant state of fear.
And when those crises happen, people seem to respond and
to move ahead with their lives.

We could fill all the pages of this book with a list of crises,
great and small, that wait just around the corner in each of
our lives. What we want to do is look at how a crisis in a
person's life can be used as a turning point rather than a
roadblock. Our growth often depends more on what we do
after a crisis than what we do while we are in one. Webster
defines crisis in three ways:

> "A turning point in the course of anything."
>
> "A time of great danger or trouble whose out-
> come decides whether possible bad consequences
> will follow."
>
> "A turning point in the course of a disease when
> it becomes clear whether a patient will recover or
> die."

You may or may not agree with Webster's definitions. I think we would all acknowledge that a crisis of any proportion is an interruption in the flow pattern of our daily lives. Like the flu, it is something to be avoided. We would readily turn down an invitation to a crisis.

I believe that a crisis experience can bring us to a turning point in our life in six positive ways.

First, *a crisis clarifies our focus!*

If you asked me to describe the neighborhood in which I live, I could probably give you only a general description. Even though I have lived here for ten years, I would hesitate to be very definitive due to my lack of observance. My neighborhood is largely a blur to me because I don't spend a lot of time here and I don't really focus on it as an important entity in my life. I am not so much unneighborly as preoccupied. But let a tragedy happen in my neighborhood—a house burn down or someone die—and my focus changes immediately. For many of us this is true not only of where we live but also of where we work, where we play, where we go to school, where we attend church, and where we shop. We seem to float through these places on our way to somewhere else in our journey. They largely become the backdrop to our lives rather than center stage.

A town in which I lived 25 years ago was almost entirely wiped out by a tornado a month ago. Only 73 of 259 homes were left standing, according to the news report. My mind went back there instantly, and in my spirit I became a part of the suffering through that crisis. A town long out of focus to me was quickly brought back into my life due to a crisis.

A long-distance call from a college classmate long out of view and touch but now in a crisis helps me refocus on what friendship is really all about. I wonder how and why we drifted apart. I wonder how to renew and rebuild that relationship. Would I have ever heard from that person if there had been no crisis? Business as usual draws little attention to one's life.

A crisis up close removes us from being a spectator to

becoming a participant. Whether it happens to a friend or to us personally, we are forced to focus on something that we would normally dismiss. We are changed when we are forced to live through crisis experiences.

Second, *a crisis can change our priorities!*

If I asked you to take an hour to write out your personal list of your priorities in life, what would you put down? How would you decide what was important, partly important, or unimportant? Once you had written your list and reread it, how many things would you cross off? To how many people would you show your list for evaluation?

Many years ago a friend of mine lost his home and all his possessions in a bad fire. Some time later I asked him how he handled the whole experience. He smiled and said, "I have learned what's important and what isn't!" His priorities had changed drastically. It took a personal crisis for that to happen.

Most of us take our daily good health for granted. Even seeing someone in a wheelchair does not usually help us focus on the fact that we are mobile. Then an area of your health goes, and you start counting the blessings and rearranging your priorities. Life and health take on a greater importance than success, money, recognition, or achievement.

A crisis is one of the sharpest sorters of priorities that I know. We seldom focus on what is really important when things are flowing along smoothly in our lives. When we hit one of life's potholes, we realize that it's time to take a second look at the road we are on.

A Christian in today's world has to wrestle with priorities. We somehow keep coming up with the wrong lists. Our world screams at us and tells us what our priorities should be, and the still, small voice of God is lost in the din and confusion of a surrounding and engulfing culture. Where is time for prayer, scriptural study, meditation, finding our center? It is lost from our shopping list or so far down that we seldom get to it. But the minute a crisis rears its head, we frantically scramble back to spiritual priorities. We are no different from Israel. When times were good, they forgot the basics. When times got tough, they found their way back to God.

I confess that I am pretty much like you and Israel in this regard. I am in the same world and I fight the same windmills. I daily struggle with "what's important" and "what's not important." It is easier for me to count paper clips and sharpen pencils than to work on my few real priorities. I think I look for the lesser things in order to avoid the really important things.

Psychology tells us that there are three basic priorities in life: something to do, someone to love, and something to look forward to. That's a simple and short list, and most of us would add a few other things to it. But we would probably agree that these three things should be very high on our priority list if we are going to live meaningful lives.

In response to the lawyer in the Scriptures who queried Jesus on what he should do to inherit eternal life, Jesus echoed an all-encompassing priority for living: "You shall love the Lord your God with all your heart, with all your soul, with all your strength, and with all your mind, and your neighbor as yourself" (Luke 10:27).

Loving God and loving each other are priorities to practice daily. I am always amazed at the flood of good things that are said about deceased folk when I conduct memorial services. I don't think I have ever heard anyone say, "He was a miserable, angry, hostile, negative old buzzard, and we are glad he has gone to his reward." We heap words of praise on ears that can no longer respond. We need to tell it to ears that can still hear and lives that can still understand what it means to be told they are loved.

Loving in family life today has fallen way down the priority scale. It is generally expressed most visibly at special days and events. But the love drought that consumes most of us between the special times does not engender good health within family structure. Existing and surviving and

paying the bills has outprioritized loving and being together.
It often takes a family tragedy to reacquaint the troops with
the things that really matter.

Our list of wants and desires comes under restructuring
at a time of personal crisis. We usually carry around our
want list in our minds. It can contain things that are only
for our self-gratification as well as things that are for the
general good of many. As Christians we struggle with the
verse in Scripture that tells us, "My God shall supply all
your need according to His riches in glory by Christ Jesus"
(Philippians 4:19). As we have been reminded so often, this
verse does not say "wants"; it says "*needs.*" And God knows
exactly what we need and when we need it. A crisis pin-
points needs better than any other human event. It enables
us to go to the heart of the problem. Sometimes that need
is echoed in the words of a slowly sinking Peter as he
attempted to walk on the water: "Lord, save me!" Notice
that he did not ask for a boat, a calm sea, or a life preserver.
His need was acute and obvious. His crisis was real and
apparent. His prayer was direct.

Can you think back to your last crisis? What did you learn
from it? Are you still learning from it? Has it helped shape
and change any of your priorities? What is important to you
now that was unimportant before? Has your list been short-
ened as your needs have been redefined?

Third, *a crisis strengthens or weakens our faith!*

I don't know how many times I have had someone ask
me the question "Why?" at a crisis point in their lives. Sometimes the Why? is expanded to WHY ME? We all have a
human desire to explain things, to have things explained to
us, or to make some sense out of something that seems to
have little or no sense. Many books have been written in
attempts to fill in some kind of logic, reasoning, and explanation. I have come to the point many times of simply telling people that I don't have any idea about the "Why?" I
wish I did, but I don't.

The real question on a spiritual basis is "*Why me, God?*"

Somehow we as Christians have absorbed the premise that if we do everything right in God's eyes, we will never experience a tragedy or crisis. We take great pride in building spiritual giants in our Christian community that we can look up to and admire and bronze. We want someone to do everything right so we can idealize spiritual perfection in human form. Our giants can then tell us how to do it, and that if we do, we will live above it all. Somehow this kind of modeling doesn't fit the biblical models set down for us in Scripture. Otherwise there would be no Jobs, no Nehemiahs, no Jeremiahs, no Peters, no Pauls. Take out of Scripture the servant of God in a crisis and you would have a lot of blank pages.

James seemed to address the problem directly when he said, "My brethren, count it all joy when you fall into various trials, knowing that the testing of your faith produces patience. But let patience have its perfect work, that *you* may be perfect and complete, lacking nothing" (James 1:2-4). Celebrate a crisis? James, you've got to be kidding! The implication here is that crises come with the territory and that they will produce a good result in your life: patience.

If a Christian can understand that God is the God of a crisis, he will grow as a result. If he does not understand this and has a faulty understanding of how God operates, his faith will weaken in a crisis. He will easily blame God for the situation, accuse God of not caring, and close the door to his life in God's face. A Christian can rise or fall at the moment a crisis knocks on the door of his life.

I have a feeling that crisis for a Christian is a time for flexing spiritual muscle. We don't produce instant muscles when a crisis appears. We slowly build those muscles in our daily lives so that they are there when we call upon them. A weightlifter doesn't enter competition without training. He sweats, grunts, and groans for long hours as he lifts weights in the solitude of a gym in order to prepare for the competition. At the time of the contest, his training is on the line. Paul used athletic analogies many times in the Scriptures as he compared the Christian life and journey to a race. His emphasis was on preparation, endurance, and completion. His words to the Philippian Christians were, "I can do all things through Christ who strengthens me" (Philippians 4:13).

What did your last crisis do for your spiritual faith? Are you stronger because of it? Are you angry at God and blaming Him for what happened? Let me encourage you to take the time to let God show you what He has for you as a result of what you have been through. It is a process and does not come in instant, microwave-ready packaging.

Fourth, *a crisis reminds us of our humanity!*

Have you ever wished that you were a robot and that some great genius at a control tower would punch out happy programs for your life on a daily basis? I have moments when I think this would be a good way to live. I could simply perform and stay out of trouble. We sometimes view God as the Master Control Operator and ourselves as robots running around planet Earth at His disposal. We can develop a fatalism that says that God does as He pleases and we have no say about anything. The truth is that God has created us very human and has given us the freedom to make choices. We can make them for good or bad, right or wrong, but the decision is up to us.

A crisis puts us back in touch with the raw edges of life and reminds us that we are very human and very special. It allows us to own and explore our humanness to its fullest degree. One of the problems that most of us face is acknowledging the freedom to express our humanity.

Have you ever noticed that more women cry at sad movies than men? Women seem to feel more free than men in expressing their feelings in public and in private. When a man is moved emotionally and humanly, he blows his nose a lot and pretends he has a cold. A woman simply lets her emotions out.

The right to feel hurt and pain and express both feelings is a part of acknowledging our humanity. The freedom to share feelings without risk of condemnation is accepting our humanity.

In my ministry travels, I get into all kinds of churches. They run the gamut from provincial and conservative with an abundance of decorum to charismatic, evangelical, and expressive. What I find interesting is when the ones with decorum try to be a little expressive. You almost want to chip away the marble and let the humanity out.

It is not easy to allow a crisis in our lives to set our humanity at liberty. Expressing grief is difficult for most people. Our grief traditions in this country are very weak. We seldom wear black and mourn for seven days or have a wake. We certainly don't don sackcloth and ashes. We mildly stumble around in unfamiliar territory trying to be cool and aloof, detached and depressed. We are not even willing to give other people time to work through their grief process. As meaningful Christians, we sometimes want to give them a biblical Band-Aid of three verses to make their pain go away. Grief, like growth, is also a process and takes time. Crises happen to humans because they are human. They can be turning points to get us in touch with who we really are.

Fifth, *a crisis allows access into the community of hurting people!*

I am constantly amazed in my ministry that hurting people are often the best people to help other hurting people. In divorce-recovery work I have been humbled and impressed at how divorced people, struggling with binding up their own wounds, can give so much emergency care to those around them in various stages of the divorce condition. Even the medical community is discovering anew what it means to be a wounded healer. Such healers draw people together to minister to and care for each other. I realize that you do not have to be caught in a crisis yourself to aid others going through a crisis. The desire to help, heal, care, and love is the only mandate you need for involvement. You do, however, enter that hurting community on a deeper level when you have shared a similar experience.

We have largely developed a nation of solitary people in the '80's. Although we work and make our living in community, we tend to struggle and ache in privacy and loneliness. A glimmer of what we once were appears every now and then when a community is hit with a catastrophe or tragedy and everyone pitches in to help. The frontier wagon train and the barn-raising that drew people together got sidetracked somewhere in the twentieth century.

I am startled by the numbness to need that exists in our Christian communities across America. We tend to respond no differently from those outside our walls of faith to someone's crisis. Sometimes those outside the walls respond better than those inside. Perhaps we have become numb by the same indifference that has paralyzed much of our society.

After an hour of watching the evening news accounts of hurts and heartaches across our world, we tend to dial everything out as an insurmountable mountain of pain to minister to. We do nothing because doing a little seems futile.

I talked recently with a friend who had traveled to a starving Third World country. I asked him how he felt about seeing that land and then returning home to Southern California. He told me he was numbed by his experience and could not make the adjustment to home for many weeks. His fear was that he would become too adjusted and lose what he saw as a point of entry into the community of hurting.

When you go through a crisis, you need a community around you. You need the hand-holders, the coffee-chasers, the magazine-readers, the hall-walkers, the prayer warriors, the encouragers, the rebuilders. You need those who have been there before you as well as those who might go there after you.

Jesus spent a great deal of time developing the community and support system which He called "disciples." Much of their training simply consisted of "being with Him." They were physically present in all He was doing, speaking, and ministering. From the seaside to the cross, from the resurrection to the launching of the early church, from ministry to martyrdom, they were present. Being in a community of hurting people is not knowing *what to say*; it is simply knowing *where to be!*

Sixth, *a crisis is the testing ground of our faith!*

Is your faith marketable? Is it the kind of faith that people would reach up to the highest shelf to catch onto? That may sound like a strange way to talk about faith. But faith, if it is anything, is transferable to other people. Very few consumer products are mass-produced these days without a test-marketing process. Key cities are selected for that marketing push. If the products go well there and draw a positive public response, they are released across the country. The highly touted "new Coke" was test-marketed extensively before national release. Test markets are chosen that best represent the broad spectrum of American consumers. The question the producer asks is, "Will it fly?"

Christian faith was test-marketed in the early church. It caught on and spread like wildfire across continents. People lived it out in the real world, and it passed the test. Many of the early Christians lived on the edge of a crisis with their faith. Death for their belief hovered around their lives daily. Friends and loved ones were constantly being martyred for what they believed. I believe that this kind of crisis made Christianity spread even more rapidly. It made faith dangerous, exciting, and believable.

Faith is seldom tested on calm seas. It is tested in stormy situations when there appears to be little relief in sight. Who you are emerges in a crisis.

One of Paul's most practical letters was written to the church at Philippi. Paul wrote it from the point of the greatest crisis of his life. He was in prison, with his life hanging in the balance. Yet from his crisis he talked about rejoicing and sharing his joy with his fellow believers (Philippians 2:17,18). His crisis was being shared in by all fellow believers. Yet so was his joy. Can we suppose that crisis and joy can be partners for growth and turning points? I believe we can! *The place of joy and the place of pain are sometimes the same place.*

Three Keys to Walking Through a Crisis

I believe that there are three very simple keys that can help anyone going through a crisis experience.

The first centers in a deep and growing relationship with the Lord. That's both personal and public. A crisis can cause you to grow spiritually if you know the Lord and ask Him for help.

The second involves having a strong Christian community of caring friends around you. They must be people who are there for *you* when you need them. Tragically, many Christians think they have this in their church only to find out that they are deserted by church friends just when they need them. Take the time to build your own supportive community, whether in church or out of church. Don't assume that you have; make sure you do.

The third key centers in what you should be doing on the days when you have no crisis: strengthening your faith and building your spiritual muscle. This involves Bible study, prayer, the sharing faith in community, and the caring for others. Scripture tells us that "faith comes by hearing and hearing by the Word of God." A crisis is when the unexpected gives you the opportunity to GROW!

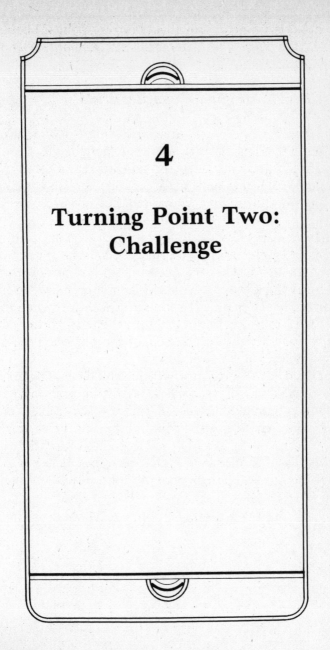

4

Turning Point Two:
Challenge

4

Turning Point Two: Challenge

How do you handle a challenge? If you are the competitive type, you probably embrace it, accept it, and can't wait to meet it head-on. If you are the quiet, shy, retiring type and not as sure of yourself as you would like to be, you will probably go to great lengths to avoid any kind of confrontive challenge. Somewhere between these two extremes is a third kind of person who accepts only the kind of challenge that he knows he can conquer and of which he will be declared the winner. The third kind is the safest for most of us. There is little or no danger that we will be made to look bad. The problem with the third variety is that it is really no challenge if the safety of winning is guaranteed.

I play racquetball quite often. I usually play with the same people. Now and then a new person will ask me if I want to play. I confess to being hesitant if I know that he is a better player than I am. You see, I like to win too! The safe challenge is no challenge because there is no risk involved. The unsafe challenge is a real challenge because we might lose in the process. The truth is that you and I will never grow unless we get involved in a challenge that is bigger than we are.

Most of us have clearly defined our own personal safety zones in life. We seldom venture beyond them because they are surrounded with the fear of failure. Failure can be summed up briefly as "looking bad in public." It is the world of egg on your face and ketchup on your tie. We do everything possible to remain unspotted.

The world of challenge is most vividly displayed in competitive sports. Every sportsman knows that his or her whole life centers on the next challenge. You cannot be an athlete and deny the challenge. There is no comfortable middle group where you can hide. Every day in every sport you are called on to meet a new challenge.

Last evening we went to a baseball game. Our team, the California Angels, was losing most of the way through the game. Finally they caught up. Then Reggie Jackson came to bat with the bases loaded. In his three previous times at bat he struck out and was roundly booed. But the fourth time he electrified the crowd by hitting a home run, and suddenly we were ahead by four runs. Guess what the crowd did—they gave him such a standing ovation that he had to come out of the dugout and wave his hat. What would have happened if he had struck out a fourth time? He accepted the challenge even though he had failed at it previously.

Webster defines the word "challenge" as "anything as a demanding task that calls for special effort or dedication." He further describes it as "a calling into question, a demanding of proof, explanation, etc." If you accept this definition, you are probably sighing to yourself and saying that your entire life is a challenge. It is a challenge to get up in the morning, a challenge to face your day at work, a challenge to get home on time to meet the leftover challenges of the day that will challenge your evening. The only thing that on some days is not a challenge is sleep. It delivers us from challenges.

I am confronted with several different kinds of challenges in my life every day. I'll share them with you and see if you identify with any of them. The first one is the challenge of the mundane and same. It is doing the basic things you have always done and have to keep doing. There is little variety and excitement in our daily 20 to 30 minutes we spend each day in the bathroom. About the only thing we can really change in that experience is how we will smell for that day. It's mundane, boring, unexciting, and ritualistic. Driving to work is mundane even if we go in a different direction every day. Working in itself, for many people, is the same grind day after day. Relief seems to be just 40 hours away every Monday morning. Raising a family and being a parent has hours, days, and years of sameness connected to it. Ask any mother who goes through the same routines day after day. The clothes will never all be washed and the house will never be totally cleaned up.

It is one giant challenge to face the world of the mundane and same day after day. One of the things that has helped me most is to simply accept the fact that this world also goes with my territory. I can change its effect on me by how I approach and accept it. It is simply the "housekeeping" side of my life—not a lot of glamour and sparkle, but it needs to be done. Perhaps Paul had a winning idea when he told the Philippian believers that he had learned to be content in whatever circumstances he was in (Philippians 4:11).

Sameness is not a problem to everyone. Some people thrive on it because it gives order and design to their day. Any changes in sameness become a threat to them. They like the mechanical orderliness and simplicity of sameness. For them it is no challenge, but a blessing.

For others who are bored by the sameness, the challenge may be to discard it all for a big package of electrifying excitement. The challenge for most of us is not to discard the mundane but to accept it as needed and mandatory to living life. It is the caretaking and housecleaning part of life for each of us. If it is done well, we will have room for other things that are bigger challenges.

The second challenge I face is the challenge of the new

and different. I have a reasonable amount of fear toward
the new and different things that loom before me every day.
My question seems to be, "Will they be as safe and comfortable as the old and familiar in my life?" The answer is,
"No!" They will be new and nervous for me. They will want
to push me into retreat from facing them. I fear them because
they make no guarantees to me. Yet I cannot retreat from
them or I will not grow, and if I am not growing, I am dying.

Nehemiah faced the challenge of rebuilding the walls of
Jerusalem. He was hurt and embarrassed by their ruin. In
Nehemiah 2:17,18 we listen to the challenge: "I said to them,
'You see the distress that we are in, how Jerusalem lies
waste, and its gates are burned with fire. Come and let us
build the wall of Jerusalem, that we may no longer be a
reproach.' And I told them of the hand of my God which
had been good upon me, and also of the king's words that
he had spoken to me. So they said, 'Let us rise up and build.'
Then they set their hands to do this good work."

Nehemiah's story is one of accepting a challenge that was
far bigger than he was and seeing it through to completion.
Accepting it was only the beginning. You can read the entire
book for yourself if you want to know what happened after
he started. He experienced everything that you and I do
when we get in over our heads. I find two secrets to
Nehemiah's success: He kept his eyes on God and he kept
his hands on the shovel. He knew what he had to do and
he did it in spite of the odds against him.

Job faced the challenge to believe that God was faithful
and would take care of him. Even though his friends told
him to curse God and die in order to be delivered from his
battles, he never let go of the challenge.

Moses accepted the challenge, in spite of insurmountable odds, to lead Israel from captivity to Canaan. He was
comfortably settled into the mundane and same when God
presented the challenge. He liked what he was doing so
much that he wanted to stay. But God's challenge and God's
equipping enabled Moses to move to new heights of growth.

Biblical pages as well as the pages of human history are crammed with people who accepted the challenge of the new and different. The challenge was a turning point for them. They were never the same afterward. Challenges sometimes make heroes in our world.

Accepting the challenge of the new and different means letting go of the old and comfortable. We are in the process of selling our home and moving to a new one. Both deals are in process, and sometime within the next three months we will move from the home we have lived in for the past 11 years to a home that no one has ever lived in. This process of relocation has injected us with both fear and excitement. We are excited about the new but fearful of leaving the old. The old home is a memory file. The new home just contains empty cupboards where new memories can be filed. Even though we have moved a few times over the years, this one seems slightly more traumatic. And there is always that nagging question, "What if we are sorry we go through with it?" The challenge is not just moving, but making the move work!

Are you ready for some new challenges in your life? Like a dash of seasoning in cooking, new challenges keep us alive and venturesome. They keep us on the growing edge rather than the groaning edge. A new challenge can be a turning point for you right now in your life. Take a minute right now and ask God to bring some new and exciting challenges into your life in the days ahead.

The third kind of challenge we face is the pointless challenge. You may be wondering what kind of strange animal that is. Stay with me. Many of us are allowing challenges into our lives that are simply a waste of our time. They have little connection with who we are or where we are going. Pointless challenges often come from other people to merely test our abilities against theirs. Their purpose is to make them look good and us look bad. It is like a child saying, "I'll bet I can beat you to the corner," when he knows you are on crutches and he isn't. Pointless challenges. Many people are out to prove their own worth at the expense of humiliating those around them.

I meet many people who specialize in playing the game of pointless challenge. It can be done in argumentive combat; it can be done in business; it can be done in interpersonal relationships; it can be done in families; it can be done in Christian community. Your question to a pointless challenge is, "What will this prove to anyone? How will it affect me? Will there be any worthwhile outcome?" If the answer is no, don't accept the challenge.

Sometimes the pointless challenge is done subliminally. It is not articulated verbally. A good example of this is sibling rivalry. Two children can challenge each other for years in order to gain the leading edge of approval and acceptance from a parent. Although seldom verbalized, everyone knows that the competition is going on. The point is that it becomes a pointless challenge because no one ever wins. Some children compete for their parents and others compete against them, even after they are deceased.

Some spend years competing against *the crowd* or *the world*. The challenge is not identifiable, but it is still there. It becomes a "me versus them" routine. You can't win that kind of war because "they" will always be out there.

Are you involved in some pointless challenges in your life right now? Do a little review on yourself. Who are you in competition with? What is there really to win? Are you frequently drawn into these situations so that other people can be one up on you? Take an honest look!

There is a fourth challenge that I face. You probably do too. It is the challenge that stretches you. I have been a runner for years but have never done much with what is known as prerunning preparation. Intelligent runners spend 15 minutes in stretching their muscles prior to running. This prevents cramps, muscle pulls, and other assorted injuries, I am told. For years I just put my shoes on and started running. That was until my muscles started sending me messages. Now I take some time to stretch, and I have discovered that stretching makes me feel good and bad. It hurts, but it is a good feeling.

Challenges are like muscles. If you don't use them, you lose them. It's easy to fall victim to the sedentary in life. You find your groove and just follow it along each day. It's comfortable and it doesn't cause you to stretch into any new areas. It is also boring after a time, and when we get bored stiff, we fall asleep on the edge of life.

Question: Are you working on some challenges right now that are stretching you? If you feel like you want to run away from them, they are probably the right kind of challenges. I remember when I wrote *Growing Through Divorce*, in 1976. I was challenged by a publisher friend to take the contents of a very successful workshop I was doing and put it into book form. Until that point in time, I was very comfortable in what I was doing. It all seemed to be working, and I was helping people grow. The thought of writing a book seemed a little ahead of where I wanted to be. My friend persisted, and I finally took some time off to do it. Some ten years later over a million people have been helped by that book and continue to be helped.

What if I had not accepted the challenge? What if I had not been willing (I was unwilling at first) to be stretched into a new area? Some of us are dragged kicking and screaming into the stretching place in our lives. We know that the end result will be for good, but we are not so sure of the process involved. In a later chapter I want to talk about how God uses people to bring us to turning points in our lives. In writing this first book ten years ago, God used a person to challenge and stretch me into a turning point in my life. It has been an interesting ten years since then.

Accepting safe challenges does not put us out on the waters of faith. I'm sure someone must have suggested to Peter when he started to step outside the boat at Jesus' command to sit down and be cool. Perhaps they even told him that real people do not walk on water. They could have quoted him physical laws to back this up. Somehow Peter was either motivated by the fear of staying in a boat that might capsize or the challenge of going where he had not been before. He certainly found out that water-walking faith is of the stretching variety. He even found that Jesus had to stretch out His hand to keep him from going under. There are many implications in this biblical account. If you have some time, read about it in Matthew chapter 14. You may find yourself in the story as you try to step out of your own boat and stretch your faith.

Jesus, while teaching and equipping His disciples, had a way of gently stretching them into areas that were foreign to them. When He performed healings and miracles, He told them that they would do the same thing. If I had been among them, I probably would have exclaimed, *"Wow, You're kidding!"* Perhaps they said the same thing. Jesus knew that to stretch is to challenge and to challenge is to stretch. Later He told them that they would do greater things than He did. They probably could not imagine what that would be, but the stretching wasn't finished.

Beyond your grasp and mine lie challenges to be accepted. If all our challenges were within our grasp, we would be overwhelmed with the present. Just enough of them are over the next hill to keep us moving toward them. Remember that stretching also makes aching muscles, and that there is no gain without some pain. In weightlifting, muscles have to be broken down in order to be built up. Short-term pain makes for long-term gain. Too often we want the end result without the process.

Challenges fill our lives with the worthwhile. They give us reason to move ahead. Scripture tells us, "Where there is no vision, the people perish." We might add that where there is no challenge, the people perish.

One of the best challenges for me is the personal challenge, the one that I can do something with myself. General challenges seem to mystify and lose me. The challenge to love everyone is often too vague and general, although I know I should work in that direction. The challenge to love

John or Mary is more direct and causes me to go about finding ways to do that. The challenge to love God is even vague to me on some days. I find that I have to know God in personal and special ways in order to foster that love. It is hard to love someone with whom you have little relationship. That is why many people seem at a distance from God. They seem to meet Him only for one or two hours on Sundays. It is hard to know someone intimately on that basis. You cannot nod to God weekly and know who God is. He is revealed in His Word and through the lives of people in His Word. He is revealed in life today and through the lives of people who follow Him.

There is a term in sports called "personal best." It simply means that in any given area of excellence and record-keeping, each athlete has his or her personal best record. It has little or nothing to do with anyone else's record. It is not up for comparison or competition. It is simply what that person has done as his or her best personally. I think we can take the term from sports and apply it to the challenges we face and the turning points we meet. The question is, "Am I doing my personal best in this area with what I have?" Avoid the comparisons with other people for right now and just look at yourself. How are you doing?

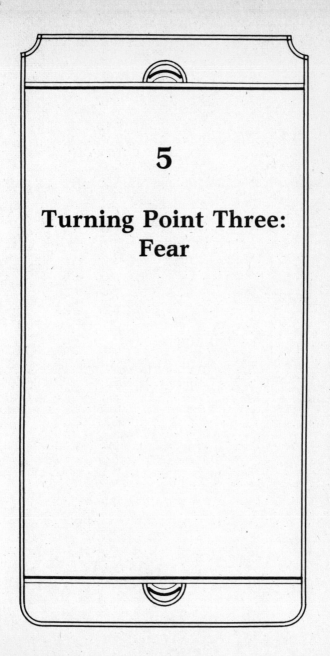

5

Turning Point Three: Fear

5

Turning Point Three: Fear

How does fear bring us to turning points in our life? Perhaps a better question is, "How does fear play a role in helping us bring changes into our life?" A little card that I have on my desk puts it rather succinctly: "When do people decide to change?" It answers, "When the pain of the situation is almost equal to the fear of the change, then the risk is taken." Fear, pain, and risk seem to have a great deal in common.

In my book *Suddenly Single* I share several different fears that push us to the wall of change. Fear of failure, fear of rejection, fear of being hurt, fear of success, and fear of what other people will think are the most prominent ones that push and probe into our daily lives. They are the ever-present ones, the tangible ones that we never seem to really get rid of. We conquer one and another is around the corner.

Fear can lock us into a corner and keep us from changing or else it can challenge us to move into the future. If I were to personally ask you what your three greatest fears were right now, how would you respond? Which ones are realized and present? Which ones are fantasy and future? If I cross a busy street, my real fear is being hit by another car.

Caution and waiting until the traffic clears removes the fear. If I go to the doctor for a physical, my greatest fear is that he will find something that is not quite right with my body. If he finds something, my greatest fear is that he will not be able to take care of it and I will get sicker rather than better. Then my fear might move to dying. Or if things are really bad physically, my greatest fear might be living with physical adversity and deterioration. Fear has a way of connecting itself to greater fears.

Many people in our society today are walking bundles of fear. We have recently experienced a shocking airline hijacking in a foreign country. It has prompted many people bound for that area of the world to cancel their plans and head in another direction. Why? They fear that the same thing could happen to them. Are their fears well-founded? What are the odds that it would happen to them? When a living fear strikes home in another person, it puts our own fear on guard.

My friend Webster says that fear is "a feeling of anxiety and agitation caused by the presence or nearness of danger, evil, pain, timidity, dread, terror, fright, or apprehension." For some of us, it may be all of the above in one big fearful episode.

Real and Unreal Fear

A real fear is a healthy respect for something that can make my life unhealthy. It is a regard for certain laws that are a part of life. I know that if I break those laws, I have reason to fear the consequences. I need not fear the government unless I am intent upon violating its principles. I need not fear for my health unless I become a junk food junkie and disregard all the laws of sound health. I need not fear a financial disaster unless I spend my money foolishly. Fear of these things is predicated upon my not having respect for them. We might add fear of God to this short list. We will come back to it later, but we need to say now that God need only be feared if we are living in violation of His laws in our life.

An unreal fear is an inner fear that can paralyze our mind over something that could happen but has not happened and in all likelihood will never happen. It is basically a "what if" fear. A person can sit down for an hour and start "what iffing" and be so fearful that he cannot move. This kind of fear for the Christian person is a basic distrust in the love and power of God in his or her life. Many people are bound up by fearful phobias of unreal events and things. Counselors spend long hours seeking to release people from their fears. As you think about your greatest fears right now, ask yourself if you are controlled by healthy-respect fears or unwarranted fears that fill your mind and spirit and tend to put you on the sidelines of life. Many people are so fearful that they never leave their homes lest their fears become a reality. Unreal fears are storm clouds that fill the mind with the thought that there is no release. Mental institutions are overcrowded with people whose fears have taken over their lives.

The Fear That All Will Not Work Out Well

Many people who deal with fear are not blown away by the process of dealing with it. Their greatest fear is that things will be more different in the end than they were at the beginning. We have been well-schooled in the tradition of the happy ending. We don't like stories that don't end well, whether they are our own or someone else's. When I am faced with fearful situations, I am less concerned with the process than the end. I want someone, anyone, to tell me that everything will be fine down the line. Maybe we got the hope from our parents when we were little. If we got hurt playing ball, they assured us that we would be okay. That basic need still rests with all of us. When the things of our life are in disarray, we want to know what the outcome will be. Is there someone somewhere who will tell us that everything will be fine?

I deal with many people whose lives have been broken and put into a state of disarray by divorce. Many have been married 25 or 30 years. They all ask the same question sooner or later: "What will it be like for me down the road?" The one thing I can assure them, from my experience in this area, is that things will never be the same as they once were. They will be different, but this doesn't mean that the difference will leave them unhappy and miserable the rest of their lives. We need to know the difference between the happy ending and the changed ending!

We thrive on success stories and happy-ending tales. They are more native to our world and to what we want to hear than the changed-ending variety. We identify with success stories because we want them for our very own. Sometimes the things that seem to work out well are less a turning point for us than the things that don't follow our rules of the happy ending. We grow and change more through struggle than we do through wonderfulness. *The real challenge is to live and deal creatively with things that don't follow the script you wrote.*

Christians tend to specialize in the happy-ending story. They have a fascination with telling other people that God did a miracle, and that if you just believe strongly enough, the same will happen to you. We seldom tell the "still-a-suffering-servant-with-the-ending-not-yet-written" stories. I think about 10 percent of the actual cases fall into the wonderful-ending category. Most of us live in the other 90 percent. This doesn't mean that we are not spiritual or are totally disillusioned with life. It just means that we have a healthy understanding of reality and the knowledge that everything doesn't always work out the way we like, and that this is okay. We will learn to celebrate when it does and celebrate when it doesn't. God can use both endings to His glory and to our growth.

The Fear of Staying As I Am

There are some days in all of our lives when we would

not like to have our game plan for life disturbed. If all is well with us and the world, we would embrace the order. There are other days when we would like our game plan disturbed because our greatest fear is that we will fall asleep in our comfortable cocoon and never be heard from again. The fear of staying as you are can be helpful in prodding you toward a turning point. You may find yourself saying, "If I keep living like this, I'll die. The future may be unknown, but it can't be as bad as the present."

It is said of Jesus that He never left anyone in His earthly journey quite like He found them. Except for the very ill that He met, most people seemed happy with the way they were. He invaded their routines and game plans and invited them to change. In another chapter, we will talk about the specific ways that God brings us to turning points in our life. Jesus' approach seemed to be shaking people out of where they were and into a whole new way of living.

If you stay right where you are in all the growth areas of your life, where, who, and what will you be ten years from now? Growing demands moving on! If you don't want to be sentenced into the present, you will have to face some turning points of change in your life. Some people have to be prodded by an unsatisfactory situation which gets worse in order to bring them to change points. It is only when the situation they are in hits the bottom that their fear of staying there prompts them to do something constructive.

It was Jonah in the midst of a great fish's interior that caused him to finally realize that he did not want to stay where he was. He had to take the necessary steps to get out and get on, and it started with him calling out to God. The same is true for you and me. It starts by saying, "God! Help!"

The Fear of Making the Wrong Decision

Let me invite you into one of the toughest fear areas of my own life. It's the fear I have of making the wrong decision. It's not something that is slowly tearing away at my psyche and destroying my life, but it is something practical that I really contend with on a day-to-day basis.

Life is living out decisions—it isn't just making them. I have discovered that one way to handle decision-making is to make no decision at all. You just sit down on the curb and let life take its course. You can observe everything with a cynical eye and tell everyone else what they should have done. Or you can jump out there and make your decision, right or wrong. There is even a third way to go: You can find someone to make your decisions for you, a paid decider who will take responsibility for your choices. Some of us have had investment counselors like that and have discovered that we would have been better off to toss a coin in the air.

A decision is always a turning point. We mark our journey through life by planting our decision-markers along the roadway. I remember when I decided to go back to school after being out a few years. It took an auto accident just to get my attention, but then I had to decide where to go to college. I wonder today what the script of my life would have contained if I had chosen some other school. (I met my wife in the one I chose.) It is fun to noodle on such things, but our decisions have sent us down the road to new conclusions.

The fear of failure always seems to seep out when we approach the decision-making process. We want to make the right decisions and have everyone applaud and tell us how smart we are and how they wish they could do as well. We allow our heads to swell just a little and wonder why everyone is not as smart as we are. What happens when we make a wrong decision? Do we advertise it? Confess it? Get help in learning from it? Take it in stride and keep growing? Most of the time we keep it silent and hope that no one discovers our humanity.

Even baseball players who make a million dollars a year strike out half the time. They are paid well even with the knowledge that they will not be perfect. When they make errors on the playing field we cheer them on with the words, "Next time!" or "Shake it off!" Somehow we do better with sports than real life. I am not saying that we should cheer wrong decisions; I am saying that we should understand our own decisions and those of the people around us.

God has a wonderful way in the Scriptures of helping His people come back from wrong decisions and affirming right decisions. Every great Christian leader seemed to err once in a while. Instead of condemnation and a sentence, learning and forgiveness were the order of the day. Confession led to restoration and renewal. And the person was not continually reminded of his wrongdoing. God has a better way of forgetting than most of us do. He knows how to bury things. I struggle with that from time to time. I lapse into bringing back "yesterday's forgottens" periodically. At times my errors in decision-making from yesterday can scare me from making needed decisions today. I have to realize that the road in front of me is paved with the opportunity to begin again.

I believe that you need to do several things when you come to the turning point of making new decisions. First, you need to seek the wisdom of the Lord for your decision. Second, do your homework (research, statistics, study, etc.—whatever your project demands). God gave you a mind to use, and He expects you to use it. Third, consult close and trusted friends who are walking with the Lord. This is not a collecting of popular opinions that you want from them. It's not even a vote. You want them to ask you the right questions and give you the right perspective, which you sometimes cannot see because you're too close to the situation.

Fourth, give yourself a time frame to work in. Too often we are trying to hurry God, hurry our friends, and hurry ourselves. The Scriptures speak often about the importance of times and seasons. A season, with its changes in nature, takes time. It is a process. Decision-making is a process. Once committed to it, you need to allow time for it to come to fruition. Instant decision-making often leads to wrong decisions. We are too used to being pushed into things by the salespeople of our society. If you don't take the deal right now, it will be gone tomorrow. In those kinds of situations where I feel pressured, I have to pass. If God is in something, He will not run out of good opportunities for you.

Fifth, after you have done all the previous four things and you make your decision, don't look back. Lot's wife speaks to us in Scripture about the looking-back process and its dangers. Paul was the apostle with the forward look. Many things he had done and decided in his yesterdays were worth forgetting. I am sure there was always someone around his life who would never let him forget what he once was. That's why his theme in living was "To press toward the mark." That's simply looking ahead.

What's the worst decision you ever made? How have you come back from that decision? Have you nailed yourself to it without granting yourself forgiveness? What decisions are you now facing in your life? What will help you make them? They may be major turning points for you that will send your life in a whole new direction, or perhaps back in the direction you just came from.

Fear Teaches Me to Call Upon God and Others

I took some time to look up the word *fear* in a Bible concordance the other day. I discovered two major ways that it was used. One gave numerous references to fearing the Lord. Many of these were in the laws of the Old Testament records. The other major use of the word "fear" was in both the Old and New Testaments was as an admonition to not have any fear because the Lord is with you. In other words, fear God but not anything else.

Fear of the Lord is best described as a reverence or respect for who God is and what God does. A more contemporary word would perhaps be "awe." Young people today frequently use the word "awesome" to describe someone or something fabulous.

Israel was taught to fear the Lord. They were reminded of who God was at every turn in the road. Their lapses of respect for God and His power landed them in captivity or chaos more times than they could recollect. Every time God had His rightful place in their lives, there was blessing. When God was forgotten, the blessings vanished. Blessing does not mean that we always get what we want from God, but that *we get what God wants for us.* And that should be what we really want anyway.

I find it intriguing that if you and I have a reverence, respect, fear, and awe of the Lord, we need never fear anything else. Psalm 23:4 tells us, ''I will fear no evil, for thou art with me'' (KJV). Psalm 27:1 says, ''The Lord is my light and my salvation; whom shall I fear?'' Psalm 118:6 states, ''The Lord is on my side; I will not fear. What can man do to me?'' Timothy says, ''God has not given us a spirit of fear, but of power and of love and of a sound mind'' (2 Timothy 1:7).

It is often out of my own fear that I am forced to call upon the Lord. It is taking my source of fear to the remover of all fears. It is understanding that God's desire is that I give my fears to Him and trust Him for their removal. Psalm 56:3 tells us, ''Whenever I am afraid, I will trust in You.''

Fear teaches me to reach out to my brothers and sisters in the family of God and allow them to minister to me in my fears. It is not that they are called to be the removers of my fears, but to be the sharers of my fears. It is hard to express our fears to one another lest we look weak and unspiritual. It is easier to hide them and bury them in our interior life. There are many people walking around you and me today who are smiling on the outside but filled with fear on the inside. The way out of fear is to give it to God, claim what He promises, and share it with others.

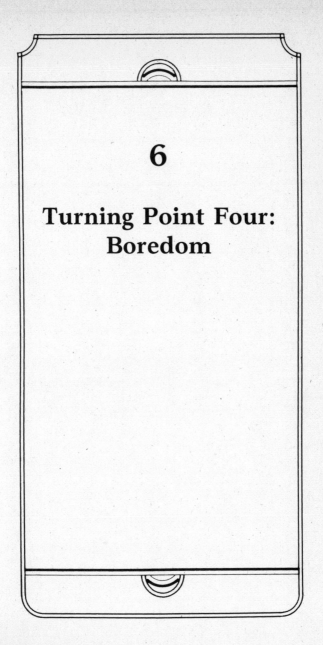

6

Turning Point Four:
Boredom

6

Turning Point Four: Boredom

What does it really mean to be bored in one's life? Webster says it means "to be weary by being dull, uninteresting, or monotonous. A tiresome, dull person or thing." If we look at this definition, we can assume that we can be bored by either the things outside of us or else we can be the one boring to others. Boredom is within and without in each of our lives.

There is nothing as frustrating as having bored teenagers around your house. If it's Friday night and they do not have a date or a place to go, they wander from room to room with the "bored-in-life" look. They are looking for something outside of themselves to relieve the boredom of their situation.

In an earlier chapter we spoke of routine and sameness and the reality that it goes with the territory in life. We can add here that it can also lead to boredom. Most of us want a life that is not totally predictable. We want form and structure because that is reliable, but we also want a dash of the new and exciting tucked in around the edges of our existence.

One of the best quotes on being bored comes from Henri Nouwen's little book *Making All Things New*: "To be bored, therefore, does not mean that we have nothing to do, but that we question the value of the things we are so busy doing." His wisdom will help us look constructively at boredom as a possible turning point in our life.

Few people that you and I know today fall into the category of not being busy. We work hard and long to try to set times to be with our friends because they are as busy as we are. We all have schedules that fill the hours of our day. It is virtually impossible (at least here in Southern California) to just drop in on people. If they are home, they are about to leave. If they are not home, who knows when they will return. If you do catch them at home, they might wonder what you want or how long you intend to stay. We spend our time pushing people out of our way so that we can see other people who are on our list.

One of the things I most remember from my days growing up on a farm was that people always had time to talk to each other. Waiting for things to grow can give you time to grow in relationships with other people. Sitting on your front porch in the evening in your favorite rocking chair gives you time to sift and sort your day and discover what has filled the day of those around you.

There are five major areas in our lives where boredom seems to set in and get rooted. When boredom takes over, it can lead to resentment; piles of resentment can lead to depression; depression can lead you to your counselor's office or to a prescription for mood-elevators from your doctor. As we examine the five areas of boredom, take a look at your life and see if one of these has you weighted down.

Bored With Myself

Many of the struggles that you and I experience in life seem to start on the inside. The best place to start looking for answers is within yourself. The easiest thing to do is blame everyone and everything outside yourself.

The Scriptures teach that one of the basic ingredients for

good health is self-love. In fact, you cannot love others adequately if you don't love yourself. It is having the highest esteem and regard for God's creative miracle... *you*! If you love the Creator, you have to love the creation.

Self-boredom sets into your life when you don't feel good about who you are and the person that you are presenting to others. Self-boredom can be most difficult when you are alone. Most people look for ways outside themselves to make those feelings go away. Many have tried the route of substance abuse but have tragically discovered that there is no answer there. We seldom take the approach of being willing to learn how to be our own best friend.

We often compare ourselves with other people rather than seeking to improve ourselves and not worry about others. We get our image-makers from movie screens and television shows. Someone else is always telling you what the standard is rather than challenging you to set your own standards. Everyone else seems to look, sound, and be far more exciting than we are. We are indeed called to *learn* from others, but not to *be* someone else.

There are many good books that deal with personal growth and overhaul in the marketplace today. If you are struggling with self-boredom, be willing to walk to the line of personal renewal in your life. Self-boredom is not a self-contained thing; it usually seeps out of your life and affects those around you to the point that they keep their distance from you. They soon know that you are not fun to be with, and you are left alone. A great relationship-building question is "Am I fun to be with?" If your answer is "No," start working on *you*.

Bored With Others

Many years ago I read a classic statement: "The kingdom of God is the kingdom of right relationships." It added that there are three significant relationships that we all have in life: our relationship with God, our relationship with ourselves, and our relationship with other people. As we grow in life, we are interacting and building these three kinds of relationships at various times. When a person is bored with other people, at least the third one in this list goes begging. We can hug God and hug ourselves, but if we cannot hug others, we will lose much in life.

I think all of us go through periods of boredom with our friends. They become predictable and communication seems to center on the same things that we all continue doing or have done. Talking about the problems of child-raising takes on all the excitement of a humming air conditioner after a while. Once you have heard it, it always seems to sound the same. When we get with old friends we update each other on our journeys, and then conversation drifts into people, things, routine hassles, etc. One of the missing ingredients in most growing relationships is creative thinking. We need to probe each other with questions, issues, ideas, concepts, dreams. We are bored by the lack of being pushed to the growing edge with one another. We tend to stay where it is safe and where we will not have to say, "I don't know!"

The trouble with being bored by our friends is that we never tell them. We simply play the game day after day. I have listened to people tell me how boring traditional cocktail parties are. Everyone pretends to be happy to see one another while they really are not. Everyone has something to say but really says nothing of importance or consequence. Everyone says they are having fun, but they really want to leave and go home. It is an artificial setting contrived to put people in an uncomfortable situation. There are some days when I think that Sunday at church is closely akin to this. (Yes, I am in church almost every Sunday of my life.) Take a moment and compare your Sunday experience with that of the above secular social time. I hope it is not the same, but from my life experience I will venture to say that there are many similarities. We need to work at making it a real event rather than a contrived one.

Sometimes we become bored with other people because

they quit growing and begin to stagnate right before our eyes. They lock themselves into their life routine and throw away the key. If you can't prod them out of this condition, you have to move on and bring new people into your life. Many of the people who come into your life and mine are not permanent residents; they are merely people passing through. We share in what they have to offer us and we share what we have to offer them. They just don't stick permanently to the edges of our life.

Have you ever done a boredom test on your friends? Sit down and write out a list of who your friends are and what you feel they contribute to your life. Also put down what you think you contribute to their life. Do some need to be replaced? Is it time for some new ones on your landscape? You may be at a turning point here. It is not an easy one to deal with because new friends can stretch you and make your mental muscles ache.

Bored With My Vocation

Since we have addressed this earlier, I don't need to say much more about it under this heading. I only wanted to line it up as a possible boredom danger. Many people are undergoing major career and vocational changes in the middle of their life today. Their attitude is that they have done everything in what they have been doing for 20 years and they now want a new challenge for the next 10 or 20 years. The freedom to do this in our society is a refreshing thing. Thirty years ago you were considered unreliable if you made a change. Today, that is no longer true. If you are bored in making a living, take some tests at a nearby college in interests and aptitudes and see what you might be able to do. Careers that did not exist five years ago are now there for your exploration. Don't stay stuck—your only reward may be a gold watch and a "drop by if you are ever in the area again."

Bored With a Lack of Direction and Goals

Are you a goal-oriented person? Do you have some long- and short-range goals in your life that you are consistently working on? Someone has said, "Shoot at nothing and that is exactly what you will hit." A goal is a target, and it defines your aim. Most of us sit down on the first day of a new year and write out our goals in the form of a New Year's resolution. Ten days later those goals are gathering moss in a corner of our life.

Goals give direction and purpose. They give meaning to what we do. They give us a reason for celebrating when they are achieved. They tell us that we have contributed something worthwhile in our race through life.

Goals are established and met through the discipline of using time correctly. And most of us could stand a daily lesson in that area. I work through each day of my life with a list of things to do on a legal pad and a calendar of appointments by my side. Take away both of them and I would be lost. I also cross off the things I accomplish because it gives me a feeling of reaching my goals. At the end of my day I transfer over to tomorrow the things I did not get to today. It is simple, but it has worked for me for over 20 years. I also keep a long-range list of goals and things I am working on under a plastic cover in the front of my legal pad. It helps me keep focused on tomorrow. Goal-setting is working on some of my tomorrows today!

Many people I meet are caught in the maintenance trap: They are caught in just keeping up or keeping even. When that happens, boredom has a way of invading your life. There is no challenge of the new. We said earlier that maintaining is important, but it cannot be the only thing in your life. You have to work beyond it in order to be a growing person.

Where do you want to be five years from now in your own personal growth and in your career? What are the steps to getting there? Are you looking for someone to do your work for you? What will it cost you to reach some goals in your life? What goals have you set for yourself as of today?

Bored With My Spiritual Life and Growth

I know—you are thinking that no one should be bored with his spiritual life and growth if he is growing in the Lord and doing what he is supposed to do. If you will be honest for a moment or two, you will probably have to admit that you have had times like that. Sometimes they come when you hit a plateau in your spiritual life. You can't seem to get from where you are to where you want to be. At other times you just tire of all the sounds that you are making and that those around are making as well.

We have a hard time believing that we don't always have to be at the top of our spiritual life, that it's okay to be somewhere between the bottom and the top and wondering if we are going up or down the growth ladder. I have discovered that I am on two journeys spiritually. One is the inner journey, which consists of what I do for my own spiritual growth, and the other is the outer journey of what happens around me. I have found that I can rely too much on the outer to feed the inner if I am not careful. I can tune my television to the religious channel and soak up what is being sent my way for hours on end. The problem is that all this becomes external to me. It can become trappings of my faith rather than faith at work. I can hear its sounds but deny its effect. It can just be religious entertainment that fills my time.

We have long since lapsed into the "spoon-fed" Christian mentality. Our attitude is "here I am—lay it on me." And after a while it all sounds the same. It is like working in a room full of buzzing and clacking machinery. It is disturbing when you first start, but after a while you could go to sleep in the midst of the noise.

I wonder what would happen in your church and mine if the pastor asked for a show of hands to the question next

Sunday morning, "How many of you are bored with your Christian life?" Would we lie or tell the truth? What would other people think if we said *yes*?

David the psalmist was a truthful writer. He talked about the times he felt deserted by God and friends. He cried out the things he felt in his own spirit. You cannot read through the Psalms without identifying with what David was sharing. Along with David's spiritual boredom and emptiness, we are also given words of hope that God is our rock, our fortress, our defender, our understander. He is our Shepherd, and with Him we shall not want.

As you take a close look at your own spiritual life, are you bored with the trappings or the truth? Do you need to go to work on inside growth and not load up as much with the external? I am not suggesting that you run away to the desert, as many of the early church fathers did. I am suggesting that you get honest and realistic with the potential of boredom in this area, and then deal with it. If you don't, you will be in danger of joining the many Christian saints who are sitting and rusting silently in the service of the King.

The Jesus Style . . . A Way Out of Boredom

No one can say that Jesus lived a boring life. Even His years in preparation for His short public ministry were not years of isolation and insulation. He was a part of family and community, and had an occupation. With the advent of His public ministry, His life took on a new dynamic of outreach, caring, and healing. People and their needs became His loving concern. At the same time, Jesus practiced the art of training and equipping disciples along with His public ministry of speaking and healing. There are several things that speak to me out of the Gospels that can help us avoid boredom.

First, Jesus was a Person for others. He was not consumed with who He was to the extent that others were merely bit players in His life. He had a way of lifting those around Him and affirming their value. He was involved with their needs and struggles. He went out of His way to minister to them. The Scriptures tell us that many times He felt compassion for those around Him. You and I will seldom be bored with life if we are involved in the lives of others around us who are hurting and have needs. It is only when we become self-consuming persons that boredom sets in.

Second, Jesus was an activist. He never dealt with people and situations from a passive perspective. His creative spirit caused things to happen. I can imagine that many people followed Him day after day because they wondered what He would do next. He challenged institutions as well as people. He was a nonconformist that people were drawn to. He seldom let things settle and simmer. He was always stirring up people and situations.

Third, you never knew what Jesus was going to say. His dialogue was anything but predictable. He said what was true and exactly what He thought. He spoke so that everyone would understand His words. His words caused people to think, question, and respond. He was no placater of people; He was an arouser and challenger. And He did not pick His audiences.

Fourth, Jesus knew what He was there to do, and He went about doing it. He never got sidetracked. He never apologized for His calling and task. He knew where He was headed and what was ahead of Him, and He never lost sight of His objectives.

The same evident things in Jesus' life that kept Him from any form of boredom are things that will work for you and me on a daily basis. Someone has said that a person wrapped up in himself makes a very small package. If you are not directed out of yourself, you run a great risk of being bored with yourself and with those around you. If you are not a person for others, you will not grow.

How to Create a Nonboring Lifestyle

I believe there are some simple, practical things that we

can do to eliminate boredom. First, learn to look at your life as an exciting adventure that unfolds one day at a time. Look for the things in your life that can add both sparkle and challenge. Too often we view the gloom and doom only because that is what seems to be on view most of the time. Second, build a community of people around you that are challenging to be with. Don't spend all your time with people who are "safe." Third, run the risk of getting out of your comfortable cocoon. Learn to live on the edge a little. Remember, that's the place where if you are not careful, you might fall off. So you have to live with your eyes open.

Fourth, don't lock up your Christian growth and lifestyle. Too many of us memorize the order of worship, the hymns, and our personal theology, and then throw away the key. Where does God want you to go in new areas of Christian growth? What does He have for you just around the next corner of growth if you will only move down the street?

As Nouwen said earlier, "To be bored, therefore, does not mean that we have nothing to do, but that we question the value of the things we are so busy doing." What are you busiest at these days? Chasing windmills, going around in circles, running in place? They will all keep you moving, but you will wonder where you are headed and what the reward will be. The value of what we are doing can be summed up by asking what the end results will be. Are the things that consume the greater portions of our time things that have lasting and eternal value? When all is said and done, will more be said than done?

It is easy to question the value of everything, become a cynic, and do nothing. It is far more difficult to review the things in your life one by one and place a value level on each. Can you work 70 hours a week as a family provider to make life good and easy for your family, but miss out on the real daily substance of what family is all about? The answer is *yes*! Can you be ruled by money and materialism but miss birthdays and family cookouts? *Yes!* Can you be too busy with all the wrong things? *Yes!*

We all fall victim to the urgent things lined up on the treadmill of our lives. God grant us the ability to carefully evaluate the things that really count against the things that keep us consumed. No one can do that for you. No one can do that for me. We have to do it for ourselves.

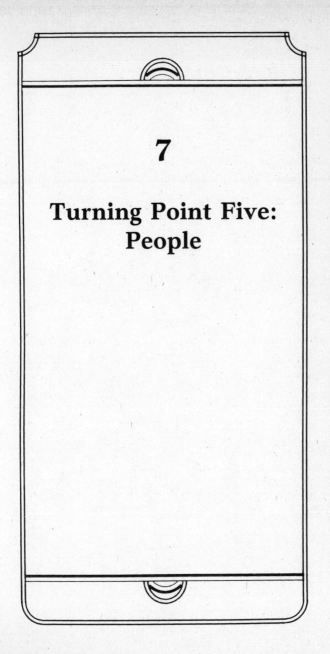

7

Turning Point Five:
People

7

Turning Point Five: People

"People who need people are the luckiest people
in the world."

After a rather rude encounter with Lucy Van Pelt in the
comic strip *Peanuts*, Charlie Brown walks sadly away mut-
tering the words, "I need all the friends I can get." Most
of us would give a nodding assent to Charlie's words with
the realization that we never quite collect enough friends
on our journey through life. We need friends because friends
are people and people are instrumental in helping us come
to turning points in our lives.

In her fine book *Called to Be Friends*, Paula Ripple writes,
"Without God's love, we cannot discover who we are. Without the love and friendship of human companions we
become less than we are. Without faithful companions we
risk not only losing our courage, but even our way." Friends
are the glue that help us stick to the realities of life. They
keep us in touch with who we really are and where we are
really headed. Few of us come equipped to be Lone Rangers
in life. We do come equipped with the need to be tied to
other people emotionally and relationally. Sometimes it is

hard to admit that fact. There have been times in my own life when I have wanted to get on my horse and ride off alone into the sunset. There will always be a fine line between the lone hero who does it in spite of the odds and the team player who does it along with a support system. We fight within ourselves the battle of the "I did it" versus the "we did it." Many people who rise to the top in leadership in our society give the impression that they got there through the unmentioned efforts of thousands of people who have filtered through their lives over the years. You may climb the ladder by yourself, one step at a time, but you need to remember that a lot of other people helped construct the ladder that you climbed.

As we move into this chapter, take a moment and think about the different people in your life who have helped you come to your turning points. Who were they? Are they still a part of your life? What did they contribute? Have you ever taken the time to thank them for helping you around some of the corners in your life?

Not all the people who help us to turning points in our lives fall into the category of friends. Some who have had a great influence upon us we have never met personally. I constantly meet people in traveling who tell me how much one of my books has influenced their lives in a positive way and helped them make decisions and grow in new areas. This would be true even if they had not met me personally and shared with me. I am an avid reader, and supreme euphoria for me would be to have all the books in print in my personal library. People, great and small, have influenced my life through their writings. They have helped me turn corners, make decisions, and formulate opinions and concepts. We allow the unmet persons into our lives through the printed word. They become turning-point people for us.

A second group of people who influence us to change points are those who speak to us through various other media sources. We hear what they say, we look back at them from a distance, and our lives are changed by them. I have listened to many speakers on audio cassette that I have never met personally. They have touched and continue to touch my life on a daily basis.

A third group of people falls into the category of transition people in our lives. They are humanly and physically present when we need them, but they are seldom put into our category of "best friends." Being a minister, I have often been called upon to be a person passing through someone else's life for a short period. Sometimes it is during a crisis, sometimes during a celebration. I am there for them, but then I am gone until called upon again. You and I have many transition people in our lives. Many are of the "emergency care" category. Others are from the "call-me-if-you-ever-need-me" group. They are "out there" but not "in here" in our lives. In my book *Suddenly Single* I identify three kinds of relationships: casual, close, and intimate. The transition people are usually of the casual variety. They are not there on a day-to-day basis but on a "someday" basis. They are vital to our life structure and our growth at turning points.

A fourth group falls into the category of permanent people. They are the people we "settle down" with in life. They run from close to intimate levels relationally with us. My own experiences tell me that this group, outside of family relatives, normally ranges from four to about 20 people. The reason it can't get too much larger is because significant relationships take time to tend, and we normally don't have that much extra time for an abundance of prime relationships.

A healthy, growing person needs to have all four kinds of people moving about in his life. If we discover who we are through other people, we need those others to hold up the mirror for us to see ourselves in. Paula Ripple says this better than I in *Called to Be Friends*: "Coming to know and believe in the gift that we are happens only in relationship. It involves, simultaneously, three dimensions: Believing in ourselves, responding to God's call to discover and love ourselves, and the realization that we cannot do this in isolation from friends who affirm and challenge us...friends who name us and help us to discover our name."

On a practical basis, how do people in our lives bring us to turning points? What are the obvious and not-so-obvious ways that they influence us to change? Let's first look at some of the practical ways and then explore how God uses people in our lives from a spiritual perspective.

Looking for a Mentor

In Greek mythology, Mentor was the loyal friend and adviser of Odysseus and teacher of his son, Telemachus. Our word "mentor" comes from this source, and as defined in the dictionary it means a wise, loyal adviser, teacher, or coach. Traditionally, teachers and coaches in our society have had a profound impact upon people of all ages as they move through their turning points. Whether in sports or the world of academia, many learners have been molded and shaped by those who have been their catalysts for change. Too often we lose those catalysts when we leave our youth and move into our careers. We develop an attitude that says, "I can find my own way. I am no longer a learner; I now want to be the teacher."

I believe that we need mentors throughout our lives. They are the people who model and demonstrate for us what we would like to be. We look to them for both silent and audible leadership. Because they continue to grow themselves, they have much to share with us. As we grow, we in turn become mentors to others.

Let me insert the thought here that the role of parent and mentor are vastly different. A mentor can keep his or her objectivity, whereas a parent often loses his or hers because of the closeness to the situation or person. A mentor says "You may" where a parent often says "You must." This does not deny the fact that a parent can set a strong example for leadership in a child. It also allows room for the reality that a parent may also be a mentor at different times.

Mentors are most often adult-to-adult relationships. They can closely follow the role of apprentice-teacher in many areas of growth. The difference is that once the apprentice has learned all he can from the teacher, a new apprentice takes his place. In a mentor relationship, it should span years, if not a lifetime. A good mentor can be likened to a wise and loving grandparent: He shares by example rather than authority. Grandparents have collected the wisdom and teaching from their own life and are now free to pass these along.

We live in the age of the lost mentor. We have become so highly individualized and so independent that we no longer feel the need for a mentor in our lives. A good test is to look back and name some of our mentors, and then to look at today and name our "right now" mentors. How many do you have around the edges of your life? Is it our pride or our ego that says we no longer need to be mentored? Many of the great decision times of our life need to be talked over with a good and trusted mentor. His or her responsibility is not to make our decisions for us but to ask the right questions, plant the right thoughts, help us gain true perspective on a situation, lead us in evaluation. Wise people have mentors and will keep them as accompanying guides through life. They help us cross the street safely at a turning point. Mentors become models for us, but not our god. There is a real danger in making a mentor an idol. Genuine mentors will not allow this to happen; people who want to be placed on a pedestal will.

Mentors are "real-life" people. They don't live with their heads in the clouds and their feet on the street. They live in the trenches of life experience and have found the freedom to share what they are learning from being there. They are there for both affirmation and accountability. You seldom see them walking around with a sign "Mentor for Hire" around their neck. They are seldom identifiable to anyone other than the one they are mentor to. We need one or two desperately in each of our lives!

Speak to Me at My Turning Point

We need people at our turning points to speak to us in truthful language that we can understand. I don't know about you, but I am not a solitary thinker. I think best when I am talking with a group of people. Things I have never thought of before seem to come from nowhere. I get mentally turned on in the dialogue process. But I need to have people speaking with me in order for that to happen.

We have all had the experience of sharing a deep hurt, troubling questions, or a decision-making struggle only to have people fall silent and offer no response. You quickly feel sorry that you said anything, or else you try to say it another way to effect the response you need. I have had this happen to me, and it usually makes me more cautious in sharing the next time. I need to have people hear me, tell me they have heard me, and enter into some kind of dialogue about the situation. I get angry when people fall silent and even more angry when they mumble the words, "I'll pray for you." I believe in prayer and I need prayer, but I don't want prayer to be a discussional copout; I want both *talk and prayer*.

The communication we need from other people is not the kind that tells us what we *should* do. It is the kind that explores all the possibilities with us and opens up the selection of choices that are before us. Other people have different angles and viewpoints that need to enter our thinking process. We need to hear them out and then think through what they have offered. We even need to hear things we don't want to hear. That's hard for most of us to absorb because we only hear what we really want to hear . . . something that supports the conclusion we might already have reached. As one wise man said, "A man convinced against his will is of the same opinion still."

When you stand at a turning point, you do not want to have someone tell you what they would do if they were you. That kind of comment is a ragged attempt at caring. No one else is *you*. And even if they were *you*, they might do something totally different. Another frayed attempt is the comment, "I know exactly how you feel." They don't because they are not *you*.

Talk to me at my turning point only after you *listen* to me at my turning point. You listen with the ears of your heart as well as the ears of your head. You don't listen with your heart and ears while your tongue is engaged. You listen, you hear, you think, and then you respond.

God often sends some very direct messages to us through the lips of other people. I am continually amazed at the way God speaks through people with objective clarity. I am continually discouraged at the way we turn off both the messenger and the message, and then go looking for what we want to hear. Who has God sent along to you with a word for your struggle, situation, or life? Are you listening?

What Do People Mean to You?

I once saw a little sign that said, "Things are to use, people are to love." The truth for many of us is that we have revised the slogan to read, "People are to use and people are to love." If you are going to let God use people in your life to help you through turning points, you will have to find out what people mean to you. Are they usable and discardable commodities to you?

We live largely in a use-and-discard society. Few things that are produced today are made to last a hundred years. Planned obsolescence has become a way of life. The new is produced to replace the old. Old, by definition, is anything that is no longer in style or vogue. Someone tells me every year what is "in" and what is "out." My children are even more conscious of this than I am.

In the past ten years, I believe we have entered an era where people have been added to our list of things. When people break down in any way and fall short of our expectations, we cast them aside like empty containers from

our refrigerator. People have joined the usable and dispos-
able category in our journey through life. Many people are
leaving their marriage partners rather than seeking to repair
and rebuild a decaying relationship. The current attitude is
to find a new model that does not have the problems of the
old one. Sometimes it is to find a younger model with less
lines and wrinkles.

We tend to use up people for what they can give to us
and do for us. When they can't give anymore, we go in
search of those who can. Those who become suddenly poor
are left deserted and stranded on the beach of life. Few people know how to deal with the extremes in life. Even fewer
know how to deal with what lies between the extremes.

People matter more than things. We need to rearrange our
priorities if we are going to allow people to populate our
turning points in life. Are the people around you special?
Do you value them as guides and companions through your
turning points? Are you glad they are there for you?

Surround Me With Those Who Know What It's All About

Have you ever had someone with no children tell you how
to raise yours? You listen quietly and then walk away
secretly wishing that he or she had possession of your five
for the next year. You know that he cannot hope to identify with you because he has have never been in the trenches
or traffic courts with you. Any advice he offers is subtly dis-
carded from serious consideration. But let another parent
with five children talk to you, and you can talk for days
about your mutual struggles. You listen, you hear, you dis-
cuss, you identify, and you hurry home to try it out.

Our closest friends are usually those who identify most
with all the things that we are about in life—money, marriage, career, hobbies, kids, church, God, food, etc. They
are also people that we have known for a number of years.
You have collected some of life's memories with them. You
have a book of open agendas when you are with them. They

are comfortable and credible as your community. They are fellow strugglers.

When new people move into your life, they usually have been on a journey similar to yours. It makes their point of entry easier in your life if the ground between you is common. Making room for new people is sometimes a problem because we feel more comfortable with the ones already there. In visiting many churches I have noticed that people who know each other best usually get together around the coffee urn the quickest. Visitors and guests can be spotted easily as they stand alone on the church patio without the embrace of their community. It even happens in churches that are known for their friendliness. You know what to say and do with your old buddies, but you are cautious and guarded with new acquaintances. That's why friends go off to Sunday brunch and visitors go home to eat leftovers.

Is there any room in your life for new people to join the old? Old friends do wear well, but new friends can have great wearability also.

People With Staying Power at Turning Points

Most of us are not well-equipped for the long haul turning points. Our instant society has conditioned us to instant turns rather than the ones that take a long process. Our patience gets stretched very thin when other people do not seem to be making the progress we have mapped and timed for them. There are some turning points in your life and mine that can be navigated rather quickly while there are others that take weeks, months, or even years. The slower ones drain us of our staying power, and we tend to abandon the people caught in slower resolution.

I need to learn to have staying power, and I want to have people around me with staying power. My patience has to get tuned to God's patience in helping other people over hurdles. In the Scriptures, God spent a great deal of time allowing people to be processed. For Moses, it was 40 years in the wilderness, not a three-day overnighter. Much happened in those 40 years that could not have happened on a long weekend.

I have always wondered why I did not start writing books in my 20's. If I had, I would perhaps have published 20 or 25 books by now. I think I know the answer to that one: You have to live life and its experiences before you have the credibility to write about them. I sometimes look back at notebooks with old sermons I preached 20 years ago and wonder how in the world I could have said such off-the-wall things. There is a seasoning process in growth and struggle for all of us. The writer of Ecclesiastes tells us that there is a time for everything. There is a time to have staying power when other people are at a turning point and a time for you to have staying power when *you* are at a turning point.

People Are God's Instruments

How does God view people? In other than doctrinal and theological perspectives? Someone has said that Jesus viewed people not from the point of what they were, but from the point of what they could become. I'm sure He felt that way about Peter when one day He called him a rock. If He would have called him rocky, it would have been a better definition of his character at that time. But in Jesus' eye, He projected Peter right into the building of the early church and preaching at Pentecost and standing before Agrippa. In those days yet to come, Peter would be a rock. When Jesus called him on board to be a disciple, he was a developing instrument with a future yet to be unwrapped. The same was true of all the other disciples. Part of their training was in becoming what God wanted them to be. The same is true of you and me and all those people around us in Christian community: no finished products; all are in various stages of becoming.

Whenever God wanted to get a job done, He called a person to do it. He never once called a committee. Israel would never have gotten out of the wilderness if He had! God has always specialized in calling people and equipping them for the task they are called to. It is as true today as it was in biblical times. And God calls as many different people today as He did then. Most of God's leaders came from the waiting room rather than the boardroom. He confounded people with His choices but He enabled those He called to get the work completed.

People are God's choicest instruments to lead us to and through the turning points in our life. God will use some who have a history with us and others who are newcomers to our life. He will use those we expect and some we would never expect. He will move some into our life and some out of our life in the process.

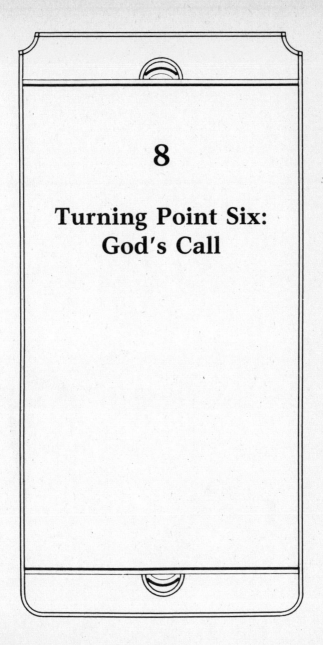

8

**Turning Point Six:
God's Call**

8

Turning Point Six: God's Call

Has God called you at this point in your life to a turning point? Does God call people to the place of change, or are we brought there simply by a series of events and circumstances that appear tied together? In the previous five chapters we have touched on five areas that become catalysts for change in our life. They are things that we experience every day of our life, and we have tried to point out some ways that these things can congeal into turning points for us.

I believe that God is the designer of turning points for the Christian. In many different ways, He brings us to places He wants us to be. You and I are not intended to live haphazard lives lacking direction and purpose. I am amazed at how many Christians live with a "whatever will be will be" attitude. They live denying the reality that God has a design for each life. If they will simply listen to His directions, they will know where they are in His plan each day. The struggle for most of us is not found in the "today" of our lives; it is in the question about our tomorrows. We want to know ahead of time what's coming. That's where God draws the line. He says, "Trust me with today and I will take care of tomorrow when it arrives."

What happens if we miss a signal from God that we are at a turning point? There are many biblical accounts of people who were following God when they missed a turn in the road. Because God is a God of love, grace, and forgiveness, we are allowed back on the road and the continuation of our journey with Him. God doesn't give up on us even when we sometimes give up on God. He gently perseveres with us and moves us to our turning points.

How does God call you and me to turning points in our lives? How does He communicate with us so we know where we are? Is it mystical, ethereal, spiritual, or practical? Is it hard to discern or relatively easy?

Journey back with me to the First Book of Samuel in the Bible. I believe we can find some keys to the above questions in the life of Samuel. You will recall that Hannah prayed for a male child and told God that she would offer him back to the Lord for service. Samuel's life got on the right track before he was even born! He was already committed prayerfully in the right direction. After he was born, Hannah took him to the house of the Lord and said, "For this child I prayed, and the Lord has granted me my petition which I asked of Him. Therefore I also have lent him to the Lord; as long as he lives he shall be lent to the Lord" (1 Samuel 1:27,28).

How many children would have a head start in life if their parents had followed Hannah's method? Samuel was born into a ready-made spiritual environment. He was sought from and offered back to the Lord. Hannah knew from the beginning who her son belonged to.

In the third chapter we find that Samuel is serving and ministering to the Lord before Eli. In the midst of sleep, a voice calls his name and he is awakened. He responds, thinking it is Eli, only to be told it is not. After this happens three times, Eli tells him it is the voice of the Lord, and how he should respond when it happens again. With the fourth call from God to Samuel, he responds, "Speak, Lord, for Your servant hears!"

Perhaps you're thinking that if God woke you up four times in the middle of the night by calling your name, and there was no one else around, you would definitely get the message and respond in a positive way like Samuel. But in Samuel's time that kind of direct communication was not the norm any more than it is today. In the first verse of the third chapter, prior to Samuel's encounter with God, the stage is set with these words: "The word of the Lord was rare in those days; there was no widespread revelation." God didn't just go around talking out loud to His people. It might have been a good way to get people's attention, but it wasn't the way God chose to touch lives.

There are some keys to turning points here in this Scripture that most of us miss. The first one is that Samuel was prepared to receive the call of God in his life. All the things that had happened to him thus far prepared him for what was to come. That's no great mystery because most of us could say that our previous experiences in life have prepared us for present challenges. But Samuel's preparation was of a spiritual framework that was planted in his life, first by Hannah and then later by Eli. He was *open* to what God wanted for him. And that made the difference for what was ahead of him.

A strong spiritual environment is conducive to meeting God at a turning point in your life. Resources equip us to meet challenges. Lack of resources leaves us in doubt, confusion, and despair. We must learn to build our strength when things in our life are good and quiet and peaceful. Then, when the turbulence comes, we are equipped to meet the challenge. It can all be summed up as "being in training."

A second key was that Samuel *heard* God's voice. Yes, he thought it was Eli's voice three times, but he still heard the voice. You cannot hear if you are not listening. Samuel lived with his spiritual ears turned on. Do you and I live that way? Are we listening throughout the day and night with spiritual sensitivity? We are really not trained to live this way in today's world. We tune in and out on God. We bounce from the secular to the sacred, from the sacred to the secular. Listen to the Sunday morning conversation on your church patio some Sunday after the worship service. What percentage of that conversation has any connection with the teaching and content of the worship service? At the benediction, the switch goes off and we are on our way. We might offer the comment over brunch, "Good message this morning." We might even think about something that was said once or twice during the week when our journey gets a little rough. But we need to keep our ears open all week long so that we have a clear channel to what God is trying to say through all the din around us. How can you recognize God's turning points if you cannot even hear His voice?

A third key was Samuel's *response*. He didn't say "What was that?" and go back to sleep. He responded humanly and physically to God's voice. His first response was "Here am I." He placed himself in a state of readiness for anything that was to follow. He did not know initially who called, what it was all about, and where it would lead. But he answered the call.

How do you and I respond when God calls? Yes, No, or What was that? Our best response to God's call is "Yes, Lord." It puts us in the place of readiness for whatever God has designed for us. Sometimes our greatest fear in response to God is that He will interrupt our well-planned schedule and itinerary that we have mapped out for our life. Remember, divine interruption can offer divine direction if we will respond.

A fourth key for Samuel was *receiving* what God had for him. If you read the chapter, you will notice that the first turning point that directed Samuel to his new calling of God was a difficult one. He had to confront Eli with a message from God that was not exactly one of goodwill and good wishes. I can imagine Samuel thinking, "Lord, could I do that later and just wish him well right now?" Perhaps the major turning point here was found in Samuel's willingness to obey what he had received from God. Sometimes that is true for you and me as well. When we are open to God's direction, we have to do something with what He tells us. As I think back over the many directions that God gave to His servants, I find that few of them were easy to follow. But God's promise was always that He would give the help needed to carry out the orders. That's a lot different from doing it yourself!

God's call in Samuel's life was made personal when Samuel responded to His voice and followed His directions. It became for Samuel a turning point that moved him into leadership in Israel.

Moses had finally gotten his life together. He was comfortably settled down in the pastures of suburbia tending sheep. No more running for fear of his life, no more oppression, no more royal palaces, no more conflicts. He was married, gainfully employed by his father-in-law, and living a life without stress and tension. On a rather uneventful day he sees a burning bush that is not really burning at all. In the midst of it an angel of the Lord appears and the voice of God calls Moses' name. He responds the same way Samuel finally responded: "Here I am." Probably if he had been handed a script for the next 40 years of his life he would have said that he was out to lunch and would be back in 20 years. The call of God came to Moses to lead Israel from bondage. The call and its ramifications were placed before him along with the promises of God to equip him. Moses tried to dodge the call in several different ways. Those ways are closely akin to the excuses that you and I use on God. You can read about them in Exodus chapters 3 and 4.

But finally the call is accepted and the turning point in Moses' life is faced. He is to be led from the quiet to the turbulent, from shepherding sheep to leading people. The call to Moses can be summed up in the words, "I have something for you to do. Are you available?" After the process of argument and struggle, his answer is *yes*.

With Samuel, his call to the turning point was a call to complete what he was dedicated to and was preparing for.

With Moses, his call to the turning point was an interruption of his life and lifestyle, which would never be the same again. Turning points can keep you moving in a direction already planned or they can send you in a totally new direction.

For the past 12 years I have been involved in work with single adults. I never planned to do that kind of ministry. My own turning point in this area happened when I was invited to speak at a singles' retreat in 1971. I went prepared to speak to a group, as I always did. That weekend, however, was God's turning point to send me in a new direction for the next dozen years. I spoke that weekend to a group of people, but those people also spoke to me. I hadn't planned on that. They gave me a challenge and a burden for a yet-unexplored ministry that was about to be born in the church. . .the ministry to single adults.

I was in a totally different ministry at that time but was moving toward a transition in my own mind—to what I did not know, but God did. That weekend was the turning point, but the process took several years to evolve. A key for me in this process (and perhaps for you) is to know that a turning point is not something that always happens quickly and is resolved in a short space of time. It is a process that sometimes unfolds over many weeks, months, or even years. That's where many of us bog down. We want resolution and decision and no open ends. We press God for closure and finality. We fail to realize that God seems to operate best with an open book on our tomorrows. The pages are filled *only* when the day arrives—never in advance.

I look back now and wonder what my life would be like today if I had missed the turning point. What if I had not been open to God's leading at that point in time? What if I had prepared my own script of life change and not allowed for God to insert His own pages? I know that we cannot "what if" yesterday or today or tomorrow. I'm just glad I did not miss the sign in my road that said "Turn Here." It has helped me be more aware of what might be down the road of my future. I want to be increasingly sensitive to any and all turning points that God has for me. Can you join me in that?

Elijah had just experienced his greatest public victory. The God of Israel was victorious over the prophets of Baal. But when King Ahab told Queen Jezebel what had happened, Elijah ran for fear of his life. We catch up with him sitting in a cave when God asks him a question, "What are you doing here, Elijah?" Good question! Elijah probably wondered that himself. He responds by giving God an update on the local news and his own accomplishments that brought him to this cave by the wayside. At that point God brings him to a turning point in his life. God demonstrates His power through the power of wind, earthquake, and fire. First Kings 19:11,12 tells us that the Lord was not in the wind, the earthquake, or the fire, but in the still, small voice.

We could talk all day about the implications of this Scripture and the operative power of God. There are many things for us to learn here about turning points, but we have time and space for only a few. The first seems to be that God doesn't always bring us to a turning point in a predictable way. In numerous times in Elijah's life, God had done the bombastic and miraculous. It was His most recognized style with Elijah. Here, however, He tells Elijah that there is another way He communicates: "in a still, small voice." In that still, small voice He prepares Elijah for a transfer of power to his successor, Elisha.

Another teaching here seems to be that turning points come after each other. After Israel won at the ignited offering fire, it would appear that the turning point had been reached. Israel could celebrate the power of God in view of all the people around them. They could now proclaim the one true God and dismiss forever the gods of Baal. But after this turning point came the *real* turning point for Elijah. It was not time to savor his last great victory; it was time to pass the mantle of leadership to someone else. Little did Elijah know when he headed off into the wilderness that this would be a major turning point in his life!

A third lesson for us here is to listen for the still, small voice of God at our turning points. The Hebrew translation for this passage means "a sound of gentle quietness." I find it interesting to note that when God wants to go public with His power, He can do it with an awesome display. When He wants to go private, He can do it with a gentle quietness. I like to think of this as simply "God getting personal."

The concept of quietness is becoming unknown in our society. Where can you go today without the sounds of the world crashing in on you? It's hard to find a place of quietness. It's hard to rule out the world's sounds so that you can listen to the sounds of God. But if we don't find a place or a way, we will not hear God and will not know God's directions for ourselves. In many places the Scriptures encourage us to quietness, stillness, solitude, and listening. Yet the clanging, banging, barking, and honking seem to be the more common sounds in our world.

I remember when our children were small and we wanted to convey a special and personal message to them without anyone else hearing. We would call them over, bend down close, and whisper in their ear. That kind of communication had a way of getting the job done that hollering and shouting seldom did. It was a personal and private way of communicating. I believe that God would like this kind of communication with you and me more often than He gets it. He would like us to be quiet enough so that He can whisper in our ear with His still, small voice. Noise can get attention, but quietness has meaning. Is God trying to get through to you with His still, small voice? Are you making so much noise in your life that you cannot hear Him? Perhaps just listening to God would be a major turning point in your life.

God's Call to Trials and Testing Times

Does God call us to turning points that take us through trials and tests? Do turning points guarantee that the road beyond will be smooth, six lanes wide, and free of any debris? If biblical precedent is any model for our own growth, it would appear that the first question is answered *yes* and the second question *no*. We find it uncomfortable to talk much about trials and struggles except when we are mired in them. Then our talk is merely about how to escape them as quickly as possible. But the call of God that moves us in new directions in our life often takes us through some rough ground. It's like that narrow road through the mountains that is scary to travel upon, but once traversed enables us to stand upon a quiet mountaintop with an unsurpassed view of everything below. Mountain roads don't really look that bad once you stand on the mountaintop!

One of the best scriptural examples of life through trials is that of Joseph. It starts out in Genesis 37 with a father's love and a sibling rivalry. It ends up in the fine palaces of Egypt with an emotionally wrenching and tearful finale. It starts wonderfully and ends gloriously, but what lies between beginning and end is a journey through turning points, trials, and tests. We view the life of Joseph from the bottom of a well, we view him in slavery and in prison, and we view him as the interpreter of dreams to an unthankful audience. We see him grow to manhood, separated for years from his family and friends. Yet each of these experiences in his life enables him to come to a turning point of growth. He builds upon his adversity, yet is not trapped by it. Many people today tend to sink with the ship full of troubles that is carrying them through life. They develop a sense of futility and self-pity about their situation and never learn how to turn a trial into a triumph. Joseph epitomized the words of Paul when he said, "We are knocked down but we are never knocked out." Joseph somehow knew that his journey did not end at the detour sign, and he chose to keep moving right along with God.

Charles Swindoll points out six principles that can be derived from Joseph's life and applied to yours and mine:

1) Life doesn't end when you are at the bottom; 2) everyone spends some time in the pits; 3) being in the pits is often where God begins to work His plan in your life; 4) getting out of the pit is often very adventuresome; 5) you really appreciate the view from the top once you have been at the bottom; 6) God has a unique way of turning pits into pinnacles.

Of course there is another subtle turning point that Joseph had to deal with in his life. When he finally rose to the place of power and authority, he had to decide if the position would govern him or he would govern the position. He had to weigh the forgiveness principle in his own life as he was finally in a position to repay his brothers for selling him into slavery. If he had not lived with forgiveness in his own life for many years, he could not have practiced it before his own family when it really counted.

Be aware that sometimes turning points can turn us into something that we don't want to be. Had Joseph let his position go to his head, he could have extracted judgment and been applauded. He could have let his family starve and said they deserved it. He could have hidden his own identity and secretly replayed the game of mental revenge for as long as he lived.

He chose the role of humility. It was not one easily arrived at after living through the snags and snares of his life. There is a strong lesson here for all of us who assume the role of Christian leaders in today's world. Our contemporary Christian culture wants to create its own heroes. We place them on a pedestal and then challenge them to stay on it. Sometimes the leader falls victim to those who have placed him there and begins to believe that he will be outlived only by his importance. Humility and humanity in leadership is a rare art, not practiced by many. Joseph certainly understood it, and recognized that the turning points that led him in his journey to the top could also turn him under and return him to the bottom.

You and I cannot see beyond our next turning point. We

may face an upturn or a downturn. Our spiritual equipment will usually discern how we will handle either one.

The call of God is a very important and vital part of our turning points. I want to encourage you to face it rather than fear it. Many people with good intentions in the Scriptures fled the call when it was given. They found numerous reasons to go in other directions. So can you. So can I. God moves us through turning points in our growth much as a hurdler navigates the high or low hurdles in a race. Sometimes a few of those get knocked over, but unless the runner trips, you will notice that he keeps on going. We need to be encouraged to keep on going and not give up. The hurdles are there to conquer, not to avoid. Is God calling you today from a turning point which appears to be an obstruction but in reality is only a challenge?

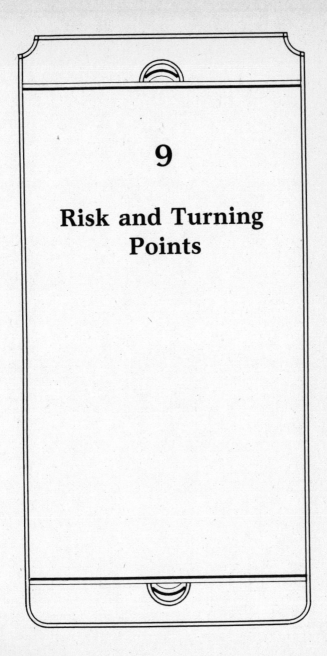

9

Risk and Turning Points

9

Risk And Turning Points

Risk: "to expose to the chance of injury, damage, or loss; a hazard."

Turning points involve taking risks. The above definition from the dictionary can scare you away from any risk that stands before you. This definition readily presents the negative side of risk-taking. It says nothing about what a person can gain by wading through risky situations. Yet our entire lives are lived on the fine line of caution on one side and risk on the other.

Dr. David Viscott says, "To risk is to loosen your grip on the known and the certain and to reach for something you are not entirely sure of but you believe is better than what you now have, or is at least necessary to survive." The known for each of us forges our link to security. Insecurity is a threatening situation to live with. Security is a comfort zone that tells us "All is well." From my life experience, I would say that about 5 percent of our population are avid risk-takers while 95 percent are security-seekers.

There is nothing wrong with wanting security in all the areas of our life. It is a natural, human desire. The place that causes us to run into trouble is when we have to risk the security we have in order to gain more. There was a time when certain jobs were thought secure. If you could just get a certain position, you were guaranteed a lifetime slot. Most of those kinds of employment have gone by the wayside in the past ten years. Advances in technology have made many positions obsolete only a few years after they were created. It was once believed that the automobile industry in our country was a secure career. People would always need cars. Yet only four years ago the auto industry floundered and many thousands of people were left unemployed. Even government positions that once guaranteed life tenure have fallen into the insecure category. There is seemingly no place in the world of employment today that guarantees financial and occupational security.

If I were to ask you what areas of your life you want security in, how would you answer? You would probably put career first, then financial security, then a community of loving, caring friends around you. Tucked in among these few at the top would be the security of good health. Perhaps that would even be number one, because if you don't have that, you can forget about the rest.

Health is one gift that we are seldom thankful for until we lose it. Another security most of us strive for is environmental security. We want a nice place to live, whether house, neighborhood, city, state, or country. We spend the greater part of our mental and physical energies trying to lock in the various security zones in our lives. We long for the day when we can sit back and say that we have finally gotten it all together. For the practical realists of our society, I doubt that this day ever really comes. We may get major parts together, but I'm not sure it was intended to all come together at some point in time.

The great danger we all face in "arriving" is that we lose the challenge of living on the edge of risking and growing. It was said that Alexander the Great cried when he realized that he had no more worlds to conquer.

Turning points call us to the fine edge of risk-taking. They put us into places where we would rather not be. They take away the comfortable underpinnings that we have come to trust in our lives. They leave us open and vulnerable to our inner selves and to other people.

Navigating the turning points of your life involves taking risks. The results of taking risks are growth. There are a number of risks in growth that I want you to look at and reflect upon in your own life.

Growth Risk Number One:
LOOKING INSIDE YOURSELF

There is a vast difference in all of us as to who we are on the outside and who we are on the inside. We can project any image we desire in public and then be a totally different person in private. I love to watch personal interviews with famous people on television. I have this insatiable desire to know what important people are really like. I know what the public projection of the person is, but I want to know about the nonpublic side. I guess I want to know if he or she is a real person just like me.

I want them to share weaknesses and struggles and joys. I want them to put their humanness on the stage of life along with their performance. Can I identify with them in any way? What can I learn from them that will help me grow? In order for them to share that with me, they first have to look inside themselves and have a really clear picture of who they are. They have to be vulnerable and open. And when they are, I love them. And when I am open, people will also love me. Looking inside yourself is getting in touch with your feelings, your thoughts, your actions. The first two are more important because they cause the third to happen. We mentioned earlier the need for a solitary retreat—time to use for getting in touch with yourself. Write down your thoughts and your feelings at these times. Keep a journal of your inner journey.

You will notice that those feelings and thoughts shift from day to day and week to week. If you are being stretched in your growth, they will be constantly changing. Feelings need to be recognized and owned, not buried and denied. You are a collection of feelings about everything in your life. Feelings need a forum where they can be sifted and sorted. Intimate friendships can offer this to us in part, but we cannot deny our personal work with our feelings. They reside in *us*, not in someone else.

Growth Risk Number Two:
OWNING YOUR WEAKNESSES

I really don't want you to know what my weaknesses are. I fear that I will look bad to you and that I might lose your friendship. I have worked hard at trying to be strong and not weak. I don't really want anyone to know that I haven't succeeded on the side of strength. If you are like me, you can probably identify with this simple confession. Some of our toughest human confessions are summed up with the words, "I don't know! I'm not very good at that! I'm sorry I. . ."

Many people believe that weaknesses are not to be shared but stored away in the vaults of our minds. Weaknesses shared can be used against you and can even ruin you. Many people believe that and seldom share any form of weakness with another person or even admit a weakness to themselves. I have found that when I speak to groups of people, I get instant attention (and body movements of restlessness cease) when I say the magic words, "Let me share something personal with you." Everything else I have said up to that point can be summed up as words strung together in sentences of differing lengths, but when I move to the personal, I invite everyone aboard my own life and real experiences.

Many speakers hesitate doing this for fear that their audience will lose respect for what they are saying. I find

that just the opposite is true. People come up to me after
I have shared something personal and either say that sharing it was an immense help to them or that they are dealing
with the same thing in their own life. I believe that human
weakness is to be shared. I am not suggesting you put it on
billboards or gather crowds around you in shopping malls.
There is a time to do it and there is a time to store it for
the future.

Sharing our weaknesses is part of our own growth and
also helps other people grow. It makes us stronger. Paul veri-
fies this in 2 Corinthians 12:10: "Therefore I take pleasure
in infirmities, in reproaches, in needs, in persecutions, in
distresses for Christ's sake. For when I am weak, then I am
strong." Verse 9 in the same chapter tells us, "My grace is
sufficient for you, for My strength is made perfect in
weakness."

God really has an opportunity to help us grow when we
are willing to admit what our weaknesses are. We all have
them; they go with the territory in our lives. Help sits on
the edge of our admitting our weaknesses to ourselves, to
other people, and to God. Like our strengths, our weaknesses
are also a part of who we are as persons.

Growth Risk Number Three:
OWNING YOUR MISTAKES

When we make a mistake and are wrong in something,
we usually look for a handy party to blame. Blame is a wonderful game that we engage in daily. We go looking for people who are doing nothing so that we can blame them for
doing something that *we* really did. The blame game could
easily be considered our national pastime. When was the
last time you got blamed for something that you did not do?
When was the last time you blamed someone else for something that you *did* do? We bounce between taking it and giving it.

It is a rare person today who will stand up and say, "I

did it and it is all my fault." A few years ago in California, a man in politics shot and killed another man in politics. However, the killer spent only a few years in jail and was recently released. His defense counsel claimed that he had recently eaten a number of Twinkies and that the sugar from them had caused his irrational action. The ultimate murder defense was saying that the Twinkies did it. Since Twinkies can't talk, they could not defend themselves.

It is so hard for most of us to say, "I was wrong. I'm sorry." It puts us on the side of our weaknesses rather than our strengths—a place we don't want to be. Being able to admit a wrong puts you on the road to doing right. It could be called confession. Confession blows away the cobwebs of wrongdoing that cloud our minds. Confession also paves the way for forgiveness. Forgiveness is God's detergent process for helping us keep our lives clean and purposeful.

I am wrong sometimes. I make mistakes. I have to admit to them and take full responsibility for them. If I hide my wrongdoings, I live in fear that they will one day be discovered. Living in fear can paralyze my life. It can drive away those I most need around me.

I have discovered that my mistakes are allowable to other people if I can admit them. I can even poke fun at myself by telling others of the dumb thing I did. Admitting wrong enters every area of your life and mine. Big people admit, little people hide.

Growth Risk Number Four: BEING WHO YOU REALLY ARE

John Powell in his book *Fully Human, Fully Alive* tells us that there are several things that help us know if we are human and alive. One is simply being yourself. For most of us, we like the sound of that because it takes a great deal of effort to live with pretense.

Being who you really are means being willing to discover yourself if you haven't done that already. As you discover who you are, you take the risk of putting that person into the public forum of life for all to see. Being who you are is having the self revealed. Pretending you are something or someone else is living with the hidden self.

Has anyone ever knocked on your head and asked if anyone is home inside? If you said yes, could you allow that person to come out and be seen? When you are at work or with your friends, are you acting out someone else's script of life or are you being who you really are? I confess to being a fan of the old television show *Candid Camera*. I was always intrigued and fascinated by people's responses when they discovered they were "set up" for the show. The truth is that the camera caught them as they really were. Once they were caught, they often appeared ashamed and embarrassed. Why? Because no one wants to be filmed doing something ridiculous. The slogan for the show was simply "People caught in the act of being themselves."

Being who you are is letting out who you are. It is taking a growth risk that once you are free to be yourself, you will find that you are acceptable to other people too. Some of us flip the accommodating switches of our personality to suit the situation we find ourselves in. We carefully gauge the situation and then act accordingly. If you are a people-watcher you can see this going on around you daily. When people on an airplane find out that I am a minister, they immediately switch their language lever into a different notch. If a bad word slips out, they apologize immediately. Why is it that people think ministers have never heard any bad words? They try to talk about "minister" type things to you. They switch from being themselves to being what you would like them to be.

I receive great encouragement to be myself from the Scriptures. Very few biblical characters lived by acting and pretending. Their lives as graphically portrayed in the pages of God's Word caught them being who they really were. I find it further interesting that even when Jesus was with the disciples He was not ashamed of who they were or what they were like. He allowed them to really be themselves. He set them free to be fully human and fully alive. I pray that to be true for you also!

Growth Risk Number Five: ASKING FOR HELP

I am generally not the kind of person who readily asks other people for help. I have tried to analyze the reasons, and have come up with a few that may well apply to you also. I think the first reason is that I am afraid they will say no. A no is a form of rejection, and I don't like rejection. Neither do you. Acceptance is the word we want to hear, not rejection. Rejection says I am not worthy of help, care, love, or whatever. It pushes me away from the rejecter and makes me feel unworthy.

My second reason is that others will not be able to give me the right kind of help that I need and I will be in a worse mess than before I asked. If I am to bring other people aboard my life and ministry, I have to be willing to allow them the freedom to do things their own way. My third reason is that it puts me in the weaker position. As the receiver of help, I am not in control. I must receive help on the terms of the other person. My final reason is that I really don't want to bother other people with my needs or problems. Everyone I know has a full schedule already, and I don't want them to feel that I am invading their life with my simple needs.

I am getting better at asking for help than I used to be, but it's still a long way to home base. I have to realize that it is only when I ask others for help in some area that I am allowing them the opportunity to be a giver also.

Along with asking for help, I have a hard time asking questions of other people. Perhaps the reasons are similar. By asking, I am confessing that I don't know. By confessing that I don't know, I am admitting a weakness. I also risk someone saying, "Somebody like you ought to know that!" I am learning slowly that I simply don't always have an answer. Those of us in ministry were taught early to try to answer whatever was asked of us. Now I know I have the freedom to say, "I don't know." Christians often feel that they need to be answer people instead of question people. We need to follow Jesus' model of communicating with people through questions. He questioned far more than He gave answers.

Pride also keeps us from asking for help. I have watched people go without food because they were too proud to tell their friends they were out of money. Others go without work because they are unwilling to ask for help in finding a job.

Still others allow themselves to get mired and buried in emotional hassles and heartbreaks without ever asking trusted friends for help in finding a solution. Many people I have counseled with have confessed to living in marriages that have been coming apart for years, but their fear of asking someone for help has kept them suffering in silence month after month and year after year. There is always someone who knows less than I do and someone who knows much more. I have to feel the freedom to be comfortable where I am and to ask other people for the help I need.

There is one more area where we hesitate to ask other people for help. It is to have others join us in praying for things we are in need of. We hesitate to ask because most people handle prayer requests rather glibly. Maybe it's because we don't strike a note of seriousness when we ask. If we are the asked, then we should say so. It is comforting to know that we are surrounded by a solid band of prayers when we have needs. Let's be more serious when we ask for help in prayer!

Growth Risk Number Six:
ADMITTING DEFEAT

Is there anything wrong with a good solid defeat? Can we

all be winners all the time? You might think so if you walk through the motivation section of your local bookstore. Shelves are stacked high with books that give us all the secret formulas for winning in sports, business, relationships, and marriage. We have analyzed, scrutinized, and formulized the ultimate ingredients in winning so that we can all be winners all the time. What these books do not tell you is that you can't win them all. On the flip side of the winners are those who became losers so that others could be winners. Winners somehow seem more important than losers. They get all the stories in the press, all the accolades, all the promotions, all the prestige. Those who lose are left out in the cold.

You and I have been both winners and losers at different times of our lives. And we would probably agree that winning is more fun. People don't celebrate coming in second or third or fourth. This makes it pretty hard to admit to a defeat when you haven't won.

I think the best learning experiences come from defeats. They not only keep us in touch with our humanity, but they give us the opportunity to learn how to handle the down times. Most of us have little problem handling the up times. The down times are places where we really grow up and face reality.

Admitting defeat helps us assume self-responsibility: We don't rush to play some more of the blame game. Yesterday a well-known tennis player was asked on television how he felt about losing. He responded by saying that his game was off, his serve was off, and he was tired. He barely mentioned that his victor was even in the same stadium with him. There were no words to say that he was defeated by someone who played fantastic tennis that day. We all know that a month from now the reverse could be true. Admitting defeat allows other people to teach us the things we need to know to avoid that same defeat again—if we are willing to ask them for help!

Defeat is not permanent. Many great writers, artists, and

composers went down to defeat in their initial attempts at producing great works. Others were not recognized until long after they died. Business success stories are peppered with stories of defeat after defeat. Edison did not invent the incandescent bulb on the first try. His museum contains the many attempts at victory that ended in defeat. He just did not allow the word "defeat" to control him or his objective.

Defeat allows us to bring closure to something that we need to leave behind in our life. We often spend our time beating things to death that have already died. We need to accept the defeat, own it, learn from it, and move on. Israel lost many battles in the Old Testament, but they learned from them and won others.

A final word on viewing the defeat process as growth: When you lose at something, don't buy into the syndrome that says *you* are a loser. Too many people tend to hide there and live the rest of their lives behind a curtain of personal failure. You fail at things, but you are not branded a failure. You can begin again!

Growth Risk Number Seven: BEING HONEST

There are three sides of honesty: being honest with God, being honest with yourself, and being honest with other people. That's a tall order for strugglers like you and me. Being honest with God is telling God how you feel about whatever you are feeling. It is living with God's standards of honesty as set up in the Scriptures. It is not trying to deceive God in anything but trying to be honest with Him in all things. Being honest with yourself, simply defined, is telling yourself the truth about you. Being honest with other people is learning to live in truthfulness in community. There are thousands of ramifications to each of these that we will not go into here. I just want to raise a standard and help you shoot at the right target.

As honesty develops in your life and becomes more a part

of you, you will find that some people will not be able to
handle your honesty. They might reject your honesty if they
are not in a similar growth level, and misinterpret it as something else. The biblical admonition to "speak the truth in
love" is something that not everyone wants to hear. Many
people want their own deceptions fed and their own illu-
sions enhanced rather than being confronted in honesty.

Honesty helps you live in freedom. Dishonesty causes you
to hide in fear of discovery. A valid prayer in our daily lives
should be, "Lord, help me to live honestly today!" Hebrews
13:18 says, "Pray for us, for we are confident that we have
a good conscience, in all things desiring to live honorably."
We echo these words in our own lives as we desire to live
honestly in all areas of our lives.

Taking risks is not a shot in the dark. It is not jumping
out of an airplane without a parachute. Those kinds of things
are life-denying. Taking positive and well-weighed and well-
prayed risks are life-sustaining. The disciples took a risk
when they followed Jesus. They were not too sure that He
was who He said He was. They were not too sure that He
could do what He said He would do. They were not too sure
that this would be the greatest adventure and calling of their
lives. . . until they started following Him a day at a time.
Their risk was a daily thing, much like yours and mine.
There were ingredients and substance involved in the process. But with each day's journey with Jesus, the pebbles
in the road of risks became the stepping-stones to change
and a new way of living.

Are you at a turning point in your life? Are you willing
to take some of the risks for growth that we talked about
in these pages? Behind your every risk is the enabling power
of God moving with you!

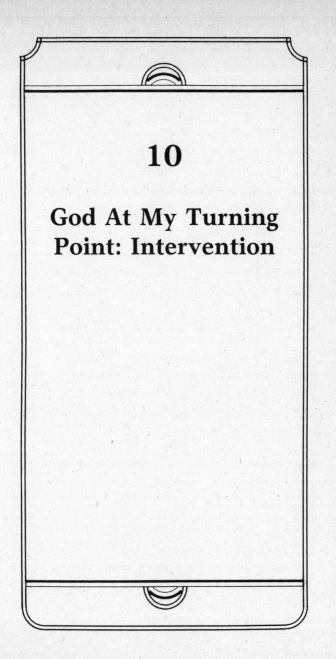

10

God At My Turning Point: Intervention

10

God At My Turning Point: Intervention

In the previous chapters we talked about the life situations that move and nudge us toward turning points. Sometimes they stand as individual signposts that have moved us in new directions. At other times they combine to present new alternatives to our future. They are not to be feared but welcomed into our lives. We need to see them as junctures that cause us to evaluate where we have been, where we are, and where we are headed. We need to look at them long enough to ask the question, "Is this situation a potential turning point in my life?" Developing a sense of introspection is a vital key to growth. Our ability to question and analyze situations that come our way will help us avoid living haphazard lives directed by a collection of circumstances.

A good question to add to our daily agenda for analyzation is, "What is God trying to say to me in this present situation?" Am I willing to listen long enough to get His answer and then act accordingly? Proverbs 3:6 says, "In all your ways acknowledge Him, and He shall direct your paths." Notice that the promise here says *shall direct* your paths. The key here is in the acknowledging. To acknowledge means to recognize the authority or claims of God in your life. It is to realize that when you became a Christian, you turned over the directorship of your life to God. Many people seem to do that in a time of crisis, but when the crisis is over they take the reins back into their own hands. Perhaps the toughest time to live for God and acknowledge Him as Lord of your life is when things are really going along well. That appears to be the time when most of us resume control of ourselves and send God on a vacation.

Acknowledgment is a daily process. It can be compared to "looking for God" in all the things of our day. We are so attuned to the special events with God that we have a difficult time looking for God in the ordinary events of our daily lives. It takes a form of redirection and discipline to develop this kind of sensitivity. It is closely akin to dieting. You have to think slim and live slim. That's extremely hard to do when our world seems to be built around eating. You cannot watch an evening of television without being constantly told that you should insert your head into your refrigerator in quest of your favorite snack.

Acknowledgment is redirection. Redirection is a disciplinary process that is attacked one day at a time. It is fine tuning into the intent and purpose of God at work in your life. The disciples of Jesus did not go from fishermen and businessmen to workers of miracles overnight. It was initially a three-year process of rearranging their former priorities and agendas. Their concentration on their new calling did not consume all their waking hours. I am sure that they thought of retreating to their former existence when things got a little slow or a little tough. But they were caught up in their new way of life enough to be challenged to live it out and not go backward.

Acknowledgment is practicing the presence of God in your life. In the fine book *Practicing His Presence*, Frank Laubach says, "Try to call Christ to mind at least one second of each minute. You do not need to forget other things nor stop your work, but invite Him to share everything you do or say or think. There are those who have experimented until they have found ways to let Him share every minute that they are awake. In fact, it is no harder to learn this new habit than to learn the touch system in typing, and in time, a large part of the day's minutes are given over to the Lord with as little effort as an expert needs to type a letter. This practicing the presence of Christ takes all our time, yet does not take from our work. It takes Christ into our enterprises and makes them more successful.''

Living with a conscious awareness that God is at work in our lives on a daily basis will help us allow God to bring us to and through turning points. How does God get through to us when that awareness is not there or has been dulled? Can God use direct means to get our attention and help us refocus on the new directions that He has for us?

One of the ways that God does this in our lives is through the process of intervention. You may even call it divine intervention. Intervention, according to Webster, means ''to come between as an influencing force.'' Throughout biblical and modern history we would describe many events and their outcome as the result of divine intervention. It is God literally stepping into a situation or life without any invitation.

At first this can appear rather scary. Here you are, sailing along with your life well under your own control and out of nowhere, you are invaded by God. Many of us have been taught that God moves in a person's life only by invitation. I believe that is partially true. God also intervenes in lives by an act of His will. It may come about because other people are praying for us or as a divine correction to the course that our life is taking. We often forget that when we invite Christ into our lives, it is a permanent and lifetime invitation. It is His right from then on to intervene where He sees fit and when He deems right.

Take a moment and look back on your life right now. Can you name some places in your journey where God directly intervened in your life? How did He do it, and what were the turning point results in your life? Are there some places right now in your life where you need God's intervention?

God's intervention is often a life-changing experience. Perhaps the best example of this from the Scriptures is found in the ninth chapter of Acts. The prelude to this scriptural account is found in Acts 7:57,58. We are introduced to a young man by the name of Saul who stands guard over the clothes of a vengeful mob as they stone to death Stephen, the first Christian martyr. We know little about him in this brief introduction, but I think we can say with all assurance that we meet him at the unfolding of a turning point in his life.

In the ninth chapter of Acts, Saul was doing what he did best to that point in time: "breathing threats and murder against the disciples of the Lord." He was actively engaged in going the opposite direction from God. He was even religious to the core and probably thought he was doing God a great favor by blotting out the lives of these radical people who followed The Christ. His own fervor was to keep pure what he held sacred. There are times when I wonder if God invaded his life because what he was doing was done in the guise of religion rather than simple pagan anger and hostility. Some of Jesus' most pointed accusations in the Gospels were directed to those who were in positions of religious leadership. He was seldom as blunt and direct to those who claimed no religious principles or practices.

God's intervention in the life of Saul came in the form of the miraculous. God used His most potent interruptive power to move into Saul's life. He used something of His origin that Saul could not explain away in human terms. I find it rather interesting that the only definition which one dictionary offers regarding the word "miracle" is a list of references to miracles in the Scriptures. This may be a very important key to our understanding of what a miracle is: It is God doing things His own way that cannot and need not be defined in our own way. We try so hard to explain God to ourselves and to other people, but God is to be experienced rather than explained! You cannot explain the miraculous. You can only accept it . . . or reject it.

God used several things of miraculous origin in His encounter with Saul. First, there was the blinding light that came from nowhere. Second, there was the voice with no earthly form speaking the words. Third, there was the blindness that came over Saul. The first two were definitely from outside the human spectrum. The third could have been the result of the first two.

God's miraculous intervention in Saul's life and in yours and mine does several things. The first is that it gets our attention. Getting someone's attention and keeping someone's attention is an ongoing chore in life. Our daily lives interacting with people seesaw between these two poles. We are always after one or the other. When no one pays any attention to us or what we are after, we tend to get thoroughly frustrated. Everyone wants our attention, and we are in pursuit of theirs. God must feel equally frustrated when He tries to get our attention daily but we simply move along doing our thing and not listening to His voice.

Second, God's intervention defies explanation. The Scripture tells us that the men who journeyed with Saul on the Damascus road "stood speechless, hearing a voice but seeing no one." They could offer no human explanation for what was happening around them. There was no answer to "Where is that light and voice coming from?" It was simply there. I wonder what would have happened later if Saul's fellow travelers had tried to tell their friends what happened. Like all forms of the miraculous, it's hard if not impossible to explain if you are not there yourself. And it's perhaps even harder if you are there in person. Remember, if you can explain it, it's not miraculous.

Third, the miraculous is God's way to introduce dramatic and sudden changes into our lives. From the moment of the Damascus road confrontation, Saul's life would never be the same again. The event changed him permanently. What he once was he would never again be. Although shaken and blinded by it, he had no idea at the moment that he would be reversing his life's direction.

Fourth, the miraculous sometimes comes with "directions following." In Saul's case, he was simply told to arise from the road and go into the city, where he would be told what to do. The intervention was divine, but the follow-up was practical. Sometimes we expect the miraculous to continue propagating more of the miraculous. We want to live in a continuing state of miraculous euphoria. If the miracle is over, we keep beating the air in an effort to stir up the miracle dust. Learn a lesson here: Miracles end, and the living out of their results takes over. God had brought Saul to the turning point through the miraculous intervention in his life. Now he had to wait for the living out of the change.

Saul had to wait three days in his blindness, without food or drink, for the next set of instructions. He couldn't even run out into the streets and tell everyone what had happened. This is just the opposite of what you and I would do. We would want the world to know that God thought enough of us to drop a miracle on us. We would want to savor it, glory in it, soak it up, and tell it to everyone. Perhaps there is something here for us to learn. Maybe that's why there are few miracles in our lives today. We don't know, or wouldn't know, how to handle them if they came our way. Saul didn't get to broadcast the miracle. He didn't get to preach in someone's church and share it. He had to sit in his blindness and absorb it personally so that the change could be evident in him before it was shared with others. Good principle for miracles!

Fifth, the miraculous eventually does affect other people. In Saul's situation, the first person (other than those on the road) that it affected was Ananias. God spoke to Ananias in a vision (a milder form of miracle) and directed him to where Saul was staying so that he might lay hands on him and return his sight. Ananias did not want to go, for he knew of Saul and his reputation. God's word to Ananias was the first clear spelling out of the result of God's intervention in Saul's life: "Go, for he is a chosen vessel of Mine to bear

My name before Gentiles, kings, and the children of Israel."
Ananias may have had Saul's call clarified even before Saul
did. He was affected by this changed life, for he no longer
had to fear Saul. When Ananias came to Saul, he placed his
hands upon him and called him "Brother Saul"! Divine intervention changes the kind of relationships we have with those
around us.

The process after God's intervention in Saul's life was
pretty ordinary for a while. Saul went about witnessing to
the power of Christ in his life. The miraculous did not follow him everywhere, but the strength that Christ had given
him did. He began the day-to-day task of being a witness
to a changed life. He did not dwell on what had happened
to him on the Damascus road as the all-consuming event.
He moved beyond that to living in the day-to-day power of
God at work in his life and the lives of other people.

In the Old Testament, God's intervention played a prominent role in the life of Jonah. If you haven't read the short
story of Jonah for a while, take a few minutes right here
and read it. It may be much more like our story than any
other. It graphically portrays what happens when someone
is serving the Lord but is not following orders. It is a tragedy
that the only thing we seem to remember about Jonah is
that he was swallowed by a great fish and eventually spewed
up on dry land after he confessed his sin to the Lord,
promised to fulfill his mission, and asked for deliverance.

In the opening chapter of Jonah, we discover that Jonah
receives very simple instructions and very simply decides
to disobey them. What follows are consequences heaped
upon more consequences. Deliverance comes when Jonah
finally realizes that you cannot run away from God.

God became the interrupter of Jonah's flight from obe-
dience. He used things that were natural more than things
that were miraculous to get Jonah's attention. The first
interruption came in the form of a tempest or great storm
on the sea. The second came when lots were drawn and it
was decided that Jonah would be tossed into the sea. The

third came when Jonah was tossed overboard but did not drown. The fourth came in the form of a great fish which consumed Jonah. The fifth came when the fish spit Jonah onto dry land. Other than a fish big enough to swallow people and spit them out, God worked through things that were already present to intervene in Jonah's life. According to some scientists, even the fish could have been normal.

What we need to see in the situation of both Saul and Jonah is that God can move into the middle of lives in very different ways. He can use a miraculous event to bring us to a turning point. He can also use things that are nonmiraculous to bring us to a turning point. The end result is far more important than the process. In Jonah's situation, it did not take him long to know that the problem was inside himself rather than outside himself. Apparently he did so much talking to the ship's crew that even they knew what the problem was. Yet it did not end with a little dip in the water for Jonah. He had to go down and have some time alone before he could get the situation in proper perspective. Three days and nights sometimes seems to be God's timing for things to be properly processed. In any case, it does take time to "come to yourself," as most of us already know.

Does God use other forms of intervention in our lives? After reading this far and comparing notes with your own life, you are probably saying aloud, "YES!" We know that God can take the bad, the misunderstood, the unplanned, or the catastrophic and bring them to the place where His good comes from them. We witness in all of Scripture how God works in and through things to bring about the "praise of His glory." But what about sickness, disease, and lingering illnesses? Does God intervene in some of them, all of them, or none of them?

There are different schools of thought about illness. Some believe that it is solely of the devil, and that God wants to heal anyone and everyone who is sick. Others believe that sickness is a result of sin in the world and that God can and will heal some but will not heal others. A third group believes that sickness is sent from God to test us and help us grow to spiritual maturity. They do not see healing as an option unless it comes from other than divine forms. There are probably another ten different views that are a mingling of the above ones.

The basic thing we all struggle with in this area is trying to make some sense and logic from something that appears on the surface to have none. We end up with a big bag of "whys" spilling out into our lives. There doesn't seem to be one all-inclusive, theologically correct, and humanly satisfying answer. I have learned from my own experience as a Christian that God does heal some people but not others. Also, many things which happen to us and around us are a result of the fact that we live in a sin-torn world. I have also learned that God can use situations that are impossible in our lives for great growth. I am slowly learning that I don't have to come up with the *why* or *why me* answer for either myself or other people. My ultimate trust and faith is in the Lord, not in the things I don't understand. You and I have to remember that rather than try to explain it. Job labored under the weight of his trials to the point of welcoming death. But his ultimate faith in God never waivered. If you ever need another person's shopping list of problems to compare yours to, read the book of Job and look for the secrets that Job applied to his life.

One of the reasons Scripture tells us that "no man lives to himself" is so that we can learn from where other people have been. We cannot copy their script, but we can learn from it. One of the basic truths that most of us miss is that we are called to pray for one another. Scripture teaches this in place after place. Our call is not to explain why God did or did not intervene in some situation. Our call is to pray for the power and love of God to be operative in that situation.

I do not know why God seems to zap some people but not others. Many conversions today are similar to Saul's. They have vestiges of the miraculous written all over them.

Others are quiet and go unannounced and unadvertised. Some people are healed today in miraculous ways. Medical examinations document those healings. God intervenes where all the scientific appears to have failed. People are called by divine intervention from a career in business to a mission field in South Africa. Others get to that same mission field by the planned process of years of preparation.

All of us, in one way or another, know something about divine intervention (if we have a personal walk with God). We experience it, we sense it, we feel it, but we often cannot find the proper and believable terms to describe it to other people. We all have something to share about the intervention of God in our lives. In the miraculous and the mundane, God brings us to our turning points!

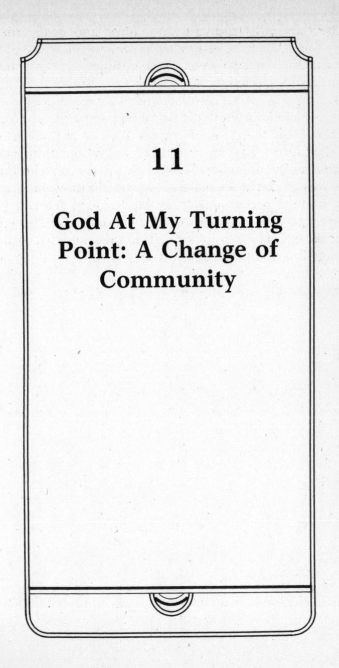

11

God At My Turning
Point: A Change of
Community

11

God At My Turning Point: A Change Of Community

In an earlier chapter we spoke about the influence of people in helping us arrive at turning points in our lives. In this chapter we want to talk about how our communities and our companions often change as we make changes in our lives.

We have all attended at least one class reunion in our lifetime. We hear two different kinds of comments on these occasions: "You haven't changed a bit in all these years!" and "Have you ever changed! I hardly recognize you!" Some people change dramatically and some remain the same over the years. Communities and friendship networks are similar to those individuals we meet at the 20-year reunion. Some people keep the same close-knit communities year after year in their lives while others change frequently and keep moving on.

The reality of job transfers in our lives causes the average American family to move once every five years. That kind of nomadic existence does not make for much of a solid support system in one's life. People where I live tend to keep their moving boxes stored in readiness for their next move. Close friendships are frowned upon because there is an uneasy awareness that the friendship will end anytime the next moving van pulls up.

As I look back on several major moves in my own life, I am aware of the sorrow, loss, loneliness, and uprootedness that comes with moving. I am also aware of the excitement, challenge, and opportunity that is mingled in with a move. At moving time I usually find myself with very mixed emotions. If it's a long-distance move, I know that community ties will be broken, and that even when I return for a visit after a year or two, I will sense that I no longer belong there.

There are three questions that help us appraise our friendship circles and supportive communities. The first: What kind of people do I want to be with? Most of us would respond that we want to be with people who are most like we are. They are easier to be around, we have more in common with them, and we feel more comfortable with them. We feel no need to change them, and we do not feel threatened by them. They are "our kind of people."

The second question: What kind of people do I need who can best help me to grow to my potential? Look out—some of them will not be people just like you! Some will be very different from you, and you will not feel comfortable around them. They are the kind of people who will stretch you at every turn in the road.

The third question: What kind of people do I need most around me? The third group will have some similarities to the second in that you *need* people who will help you reach your potential. But you also have some other needs in people. You need affirmers, encouragers, questioners, challengers, and helpers. They will not all come packaged in one person. Those needs will be met through a collection of people in your life. Let me add two other questions here: What kind of people do I *not* want to be around, and what kind of people will help me grow spiritually? Most of us don't have a problem with the first question because we react quickly to people we don't want or need in our communities. But some sneak into our lives anyway, and we have to realize that they are not healthy for us to be around. Most of us hate to be around people who are negative and complaining all the time. We know that their negativism can have a toxic effect on our own lives if we are around them very much.

Most of us do not stop long enough to evaluate our friendship circles on the basis of these three questions. If we did, some of our structures would change radically. We would bring new people into our lives that would stimulate and challenge us as well as affirm and encourage us. Many people suffer from the tired-relationships syndrome. The people that they cling to offer very little by way of challenge and newness to their lives. If they could be honest, they might say that they are bored with their friends and need to move out and expand their community. Reluctance in doing this stems from the fact that this is work, and that it is easier to stay with the boredom of predictability than to face the challenge of change.

Our communities of friends exist in many areas of our lives. A dramatic shift has taken place in our personal communities in the past 10 to 20 years. There was a time when community meant the street where you live, the neighborhood or town where you live. Our relational center was focused on the people around us in that area. But in many places in our country today, that has changed. The new focus of community is where we work. Recreation and further education is tied to our workplace. Children are even involved in preschool structures in the new workplace. Cafeterias and gyms remind us of our years in college. The only difference is that our dormitory room is out in suburbia somewhere, and we go there when it gets dark and leave there when it starts to get light. Large companies take pride in the fact that they supply everything for you if you work for them. Japanese industry and technology has led the way in this environmental change. How can you coach Little

League in your community if you are bowling with your company?

At one time the local school and church formed the frameworks of relational structure in our lives. That time is slipping away with each passing year. Many marriages are in a state of decay because both partners work, and more time awake is spent building friendships in the workplace than in cementing husband-wife ties by the fireplace.

Much has been written lately about the loss of community in our culture. We build more and more communities but have less and less community. Turning points are good places to look at and evaluate your companions in community. Be thinking about your own structures as you work your way through this chapter.

You and I have two very different kinds of communities at work in our lives. We have our non-Christian friends and our Christian friends. We usually refer to them as those we work with and those we go to church with. They comprise two distinctly different groups of people in our lives. If our Christian commitment is real, we are trying to introduce our non-Christian friends to a personal faith in Jesus Christ and move them into our Christian-friends circle. This is usually more difficult than it sounds, and often we simply choose to relate to two very segregated groups in our lives.

Coming to a turning point with your Christian community is asking the question, "Are these people helping me grow spiritually?" Paul's word regarding the obligation of Christian community to help others grow is found in 1 Thessalonians 5:11: "Comfort each other and edify one another, just as you also are doing." "Comfort" and "edify" are process words tied to community. Is your Christian community encouraging and building you in your spiritual life? I have come to a recent conclusion that there is a vast difference in the *observance* of spiritual growth and the *ministry* of spiritual growth. The first involves being a spectator; the second involves being a participant. Ministry is something that one *does*; it is an act of involvement with other people.

Paul practiced the Christian life in the trenches alongside his fellow strugglers. He was doing and being regardless of where he was. He was constantly encouraging and building up others in their faith. They in turn did the same for him. This is the finest form of ministry there is.

Many churches today can be compared with the classic definition of the game of football. . .fifty thousand people in the stands in need of exercise and 22 people on the field in need of rest! The crowds that jam our churches on any given Sunday across America are in desperate need of exercising their faith. The hired church staff has been doing that all week, and they are in need of a day or two off. Growth is always contagious. If you and I are to experience it, we must be where it is happening. Now I am not advocating that everyone go church-shopping at this juncture, but I am suggesting that you ask the question, "Are these people helping me grow spiritually?" And I am suggesting that you quit asking this question just of the one man who preaches from your pulpit, and instead ask it of the entire collection of believers that surround your life.

I used to hesitate when people told me they were not growing spiritually in their church and asked if they should leave. I used to tell them to hang in there and try to change things. Not anymore. If you have done all you can do but are not continuing to grow, you will die and fall into the dead space occupied by other people. When you look for a new church home, look for a place where it doesn't all happen within the church walls but is happening all over town as a result of what's emanating from the church.

What Should Be Happening in Your Christian Community?

How do you evaluate what should be taking place in your Christian community if you are to be living on the growing edge of your faith? Many people look to the organizational things, such as good music, good youth programs, good educational programs, exciting worship services, etc. These things are important, as we all know, but there are important "inside" ingredients that support and contribute to our growth in community. If you want a measuring stick for your community, here it is in the form of seven biblical admonitions.

1. *Accept one another.* Romans 15:7 says, "Receive one another, just as Christ also received us to the glory of God." It is usually difficult to find your way into a new Christian community. You attend, stand around, look interested, and hope someone will talk with you. You want to say, "Here I am! I need you! Will you accept me?" I am firmly convinced that many thousands of visitors leave churches every Sunday with their mind made up that they will not be accepted there. Acceptance is no overnight or coffeetime-on-the-patio quickie. It takes time to know and be known. Basic acceptance takes many different forms. Jesus practiced His style of acceptance throughout His ministry in the Gospels. Read them and discover how He did it. He did not just accept those who were most like Him and the disciples. His pendulum of acceptance swung from the sick and destitute to the politician and prostitute. He even included children, much to the dismay of the disciples. Acceptance should be followed with the words "Just as you are!"

2. *Love one another.* John 13:34 tells us, "A new commandment I give to you, that you love one another; as I have loved you, that you also love one another." These words were initially shared in private with the disciples. It was a good housekeeping mandate. They were to embody it relationally with one another before they were to practice it in public. They might have wondered if it would not have been easier to start with the public part first, since the general is usually easier than the specific. Loving follows hard on the heels of accepting. It initiates the "hands-on" principle of caring that Jesus tried to teach His disciples. It was loving

up close, not at a distance. It was loving those who were not the easiest to love. It was loving those they knew best.

3. *Bear others' burdens*. Galatians 6:2 says, "Bear one another's burdens, and so fulfill the law of Christ." What is the law of Christ? To love one another. If that law is a mandate to you and me in Christian community, then we carry it out through the process of bearing one another's burdens. Notice that this Scripture does not say *remove* the burdens of someone else. It says *bear*. "Bear" means to assist in carrying, to allow some of the weight to fall on your shoulders while you walk alongside hurting persons. The early Christians excelled in this area. They knew the spirit of community caring better than most. They knew that if they did not do this, they would all crumble.

You and I are not called to bear everyone's burdens, or else we would falter and wilt under the load. I believe that God calls us alongside certain people to assist in their process of burden-bearing. When He calls you to this, respond. We will be more gifted in helping with some people than with others. Our call is to be there for them in their need. Sometimes the *being* there is far more important than the *doing* while there.

4. *Forgive one another*. Ephesians 4:32 encourages us to "be kind to one another, tenderhearted, forgiving one another, just as God in Christ also forgave you." Forgiveness is the glue that holds us together in community. Without it there would be no such thing as community. Forgiveness was included in the Lord's prayer and was publicly proclaimed from the cross. Forgiveness is the most needed thing in Christian community, and the toughest to deal with. You have to give it in order to get it. It is constant, daily, and continuing in our lives. We deal with it on three fronts: God forgives me, I forgive myself, and I forgive others. We often use the words "I'm sorry" to illustrate desired forgiveness. We know that once we have

experienced it, we are fresh, clean, and renewed.

5. *Teach and admonish one another.* Colossians 3:16 says, "Let the word of Christ dwell in you richly in all wisdom, teaching and admonishing one another in psalms and hymns and spiritual songs, singing with grace in your hearts to the Lord." Nourishing one another in spiritual growth is a directive for living in Christian community. The responsibility for doing this does not rest solely upon a pastor or a church staff; it rests upon all of us all of the time. In order to teach, you have to be with someone in the wide spectrum of life's experiences. It is not just confined to a classroom with teacher and Bible study material. That's one small dimension of teaching. Jesus did very little with the disciples in formal instruction. He had a few intimate chats with them, but most of the time they were simply *with Him.* In being with Him, they learned who He was and what He was all about. From temple to hillside to seaside to roadside, they were *with Him.* Teaching by example is more what the letter to the Colossians had in mind. The admonish part means to urge, warn, and correct those who were not too willing to receive the teaching that community offered to them. It may well have applied to those who were negligent or hesitant to be as involved in community as was needed for them.

6. *Esteem others above yourself.* Philippians 2:3 teaches, "Let nothing be done through selfish ambition or conceit, but in lowliness of mind let each esteem others better than himself." In simple translation this verse means "Know who you are." If you know who you are, you will know who others are and how to treat them. One of the greatest battles we fight on the inside of Christian community is the ego war. Because we are human, we want our ego fanned by the gentle breezes of applause and recognition. For some people there is never enough. Others are in the business of filling the skies with their own press releases.

The secret to being important is in how we treat other

people. We are not instructed to climb over each other in
order to get to the top; we are told to defer to others. This
teaching seems to be almost forgotten in Christian community today. "My church is bigger and better than your
church" or "My life is bigger and more important than your
life" echo out to us from the canyons of Christian community today. Work on just knowing who you are, and forget
the noise around you. Humility can qualify as a contemporary Christian lifestyle today.

7. *Serve one another.* First Peter 4:10 states, "As each one
has received a gift, minister it to one another, as good
stewards of the manifold grace of God." This Scripture
implies that you and I are possessors of a spiritual gift or
gifts. The Scriptures list a total of about 22 such gifts, and
indicate that these gifts are given to different Christians in
differing quantities so that we can serve one another with
them. What this verse says between the lines is that you
and I are servants. That's where we start from. At times we
are serving and at other times we are being served with the
gifts of others. It puts us on both ends of the servant
spectrum. We said earlier that it is difficult to be a receiver
of gifts because it takes us out of the control position. It is
also difficult to be a server of a gift because the servant side
of our society is looked upon as the lesser side. If you don't
believe that, just watch the waitress-customer rapport the
next time you are in a restaurant. Jesus came to His public
ministry in the garb of a servant. He did not come to be
waited upon. He came to do the waiting. He emulated this
in His ministry with the disciples. He encouraged no special treatment of Himself. His was the mission of a servant,
and you and I are called to the same thing.

These are seven principles from Scripture which could
simply be called the "one another" principles. They cannot succeed on a *one only* basis; they become operative in
community. Are these principles operative in your Chris-

tian community? Do they function first in your inner circle of Christian friends? Do they then carry from there to your larger church body? Do you see these things visibly taking place week by week as your body of believers intertwine their lives together?

Turning points come when people commit to this kind of life together. Our communities have their different breakdowns and catalysts. We move from one to another as we make decisions in our lives. The ingredients of our community structures change from time to time, and for each of us that is healthy growth. Saul, who became Paul, watched his own change right before his own eyes. Those he once persecuted now stood with him as he preached and witnessed to his new faith in Christ. It probably felt strange for both parties as he moved closer and deeper into the early Christian network. As he said to the church at Corinth, "If anyone is in Christ, he is a new creation; old things have passed away; behold, all things have become new" (2 Corinthians 5:17). Part of this new creation for Paul was the creation of a new community. Some of you reading this have had the same experience at the point of conversion.

As the disciples were called to follow Jesus, their communities changed. They went new places with new friends and made new discoveries. When called to lead Israel from bondage, Moses left his old community and established a new one. We could say that God seems to be always calling us out of and toward new relationships and new communities.

Is God calling you to the turning point of a new community and new friendships? Is it time to let go of things that are no longer helping you grow and people who are blocking instead of nurturing your spiritual journey?

12

God At My Turning Point: A Change of Direction

12

God At My Turning Point: A Change Of Direction

A few weeks ago I again fell victim to one of my subtle weaknesses. I was to visit a new doctor, and the receptionist asked me on the telephone if I needed directions to the office. Since I knew the general area where the office was, I told her I did not need her help. I left my office later than I should have to keep my appointment. I went to the location I thought the office was in, only to find that it wasn't there. After 15 minutes of futile racing about, I finally found it and arrived in a harried and shredded state. As I sat in the waiting room I thought that this could have been avoided if only I had taken a moment to write down directions offered by the secretary.

Asking for and receiving directions is a real responsibility if I am to navigate my way through life. Many people have the same problem I have. They want to appear wise, informed, educated, and in charge. They want to project the image that they always know what they are doing and where they are going. To a person like that, anyone asking questions for directions just gets in our way.

I am learning that you get things done better, faster, and smarter if you take the time to ask someone who is better informed than you are, and then follow what he or she tells you. I stand in awe of people who seem to know something about everything. Then I find out that they are the kind of people who are willing to project their lack of knowledge by asking questions that will help them gain knowledge. If you are a receiver of directions, you are qualified to offer directions.

A change of direction in a person's life involves receiving directions that are asked for. It also means that there is a willingness to alter a life course and head in a totally new direction. Many people are going back to school in midlife today because they want to pursue a whole new vocational direction. It is no longer strange to see a mother and daughter in the same graduating class. Evening school courses at colleges are heavily populated with older adults who are moving in a new direction.

One of the biggest things that we all face in considering a new direction in any area of our life is the enigma of fear. The other day I tried to put together a list of fears for my life and yours that are relevant to this area. I want to share them with you and try to pop these balloons of fear so that you can make the choices for change in your own life.

1. *I might fail!* I know I will fail! The fear of failure looms large in any area of change in our lives. If we could fail privately and no one else would ever know about it, we would be fine. It is failure that is witnessed in public that haunts us most. One of our greatest freedoms is the freedom to fail. I will grant that it is by far the most unpopular one. No one really wants to fall victim to it, but every batter who strikes out in baseball is really a failure that time at bat. But somehow, as the batting rotation comes around, that same batter comes up and the crowd cheers for what they hope he will do this time around. The last strike out is soon forgotten when a base hit is obtained. We need to learn that failure is merely a test of where we are in our growth. It is never intended as a permanent stigma to put us on the sidelines

of life. You have the freedom to fail!

2. *I'll look stupid!* No one wants to look bad at anything, anywhere, anytime. We work extra hard trying to do the things that make us look good and avoiding the things that make us look bad. A change in direction in our life is always risking that we might look stupid to other people as well as ourselves. We all have people tossing that marvelous statement at us every day, "If I were you, I wouldn't do that!" Or, "If you do that, you'll be sorry!" First, they are not you, so the statement is pointless. Second, they haven't the slightest proof that you will be sorry for what you're doing unless it is some very evil deed and God guarantees that you will receive His wrath. One of the things that helps us avoid the fear of looking stupid is to have the innate ability to laugh at ourselves once in a while. If you are the first to admit you have made a wrong move and can laugh about it, you will disarm your opposition.

3. *I might get hurt!* I think that coming to the turning point of a new direction in any area of your life is painful. Some of that pain comes from the experience itself and some from the situations and people attending the experience. We fear hurt primarily because of the pain associated with it. If hurt caused us to have no emotional response, it would not be a problem. We live with bruised emotions every day of our life. We often feel like the fruit in the supermarket being squeezed by the shoppers as they pass by. Hurt goes with changes of direction, because you cannot please everyone. On some days it is difficult to please even yourself.

4. *People won't like me!* We work very hard in life trying to obtain the self-esteem we need by getting other people to like us. We can work at it so feverishly that we end up playing out our whole life to the people in the audience of life. After a while they dictate to us what we are to do and be in order to please them. People-pleasers really end up

in a game they cannot win because there are too many people out there to please and you will always be playing catch-
up. I discovered a long time ago that not everyone likes me
or understands me. This is true even inside the Christian
circles that most of us live our lives in. It is true even though
the Scriptures tell us to love each other. Not everyone likes
you and not everyone likes me. That can be quite a shock,
but if you accept it, you will not be caught in any people-
pleaser traps. People won't always cheer your change of
direction in life. They often question and demean your decision. Much of that comes from jealousy and envy that you
are doing what they wished they could do. There are only
scattered cheers for those who are strong enough to change
course in life.

5. *I'll lose everything!* We are currently going through the
worst siege of brush fires in California history. As I watch
I see and hear despair and defeat in the voices and faces
of many people as they respond to the interviewer's questions. In the faces of others I see a faint smile and hear the
response that they have not really lost everything because
they and their families are alive and have the hope of tomorrow and rebuilding. We cheer for the courageous and have
empathy for the defeated. We also know that each of us can
lose something when we move in a new direction in our
lives. We seldom lose everything, even in a bad decision.
We always lose something, but some things that are lost
should be lost. New things will always take their place. The
thought of losing everything is a vacuum-cleaner fear that
takes in everything but never really happens. Reality says
that you will lose some things. That is always the cost of
change.

6. *I might lose my job!* To most people, a good job is the
most readily accepted form of security in our society. With
the job comes income, and with income we can pay our bills
and pursue our lifestyle. Loss of job is often a violent inter-

ruption of our lives. It is feared by many. Changing direction can mean a change in your job. It may well go with the territory as a needed change for you. It is not something to be feared, because fear in this area can cause a paralysis in other needed areas of change. My father used to say that there is always a job for those who will work. In today's world many people will not work for survival but only for the job they feel they deserve.

7. *God will be angry with me!* Many people fear that God will not be with them in their new directions. That is true only if you are living outside the will of God for your life. Sometimes I think we have made the will of God some meticulously long list of things similar to a contract we sign when we buy a house. I believe the will of God is very basic in our lives. The Westminster Confession of Faith tells us, "The chief end of man is to glorify God and serve Him forever." The Scriptures portray this over and over. I once asked a friend of mine about geography and the will of God. Does God really have only one place at a time that you can live and be happy? If you live anywhere else, will God bless you? His response was, "God doesn't really care where you live. He cares that you are faithful." That may sound like a very broad extreme, but I think he is on target. I could minister in my work in thousands of different places in this country and experience the blessing of God. But I know that I prefer living in a warm climate as opposed to a cold one, and I don't think this bothers God at all. The same is true in how we make our living, where we attend church, etc. I believe that there are "best" places for us at any particular time, but I question ultimate places. The anger of God is not directed at those who are seeking His leading in their lives.

8. *Something bad will happen!* Do you ever have a week or month when you feel you are on a roll? Everything seems to fall in place and go right. You are simply amazed that

things are going so well. Then, all of a sudden, you start thinking that something bad will happen because these good things just can't keep happening to you forever. You begin looking under bushes and around corners for the bad stuff. You even look for the bad in the good. Many of us live that way, and I'm not sure why. Maybe it's because we feel we don't really deserve goodness on any continuing basis. It also might have something to do with our conception of God. If we believe that God is a stern father-figure who delights in doling out punishment, we will be cringing before Him in our lives waiting for the bad to rain upon us. If we believe that God is a God of love and desires good things for His children, we will rejoice when the good comes to us. We can live with the fear that something bad lurks around the next corner, or else we can live in trust that God is around the corner with whatever awaits us in our journey.

9. *I'll feel guilty!* Do you feel guilty when you make right decisions in your life? Do you feel guilty when you make wrong ones and end up a long way down the road of wrong directions? If you are fairly normal, the answers would be *no* to the first question and *yes* to the second. Guilt is an emotional tide that can sweep into our life and drown us in a sea of self-pity. Guilt causes us to feel sorry at situations we often cannot change. When we are overwhelmed with self-pity, depression usually sets in and pushes us into a corner in our lives.

Guilt says, "I wish I had not done that, but I did." The only genuine relief for guilt is confession and forgiveness. It can lead us to a fresh start. Sometimes you can feel guilty when you choose right directions. Your guilt can be centered in the fact that other people were not able to make the same decision and share in your joy.

Guilt can sometimes introduce honesty into your life in a new way. Honesty is the by-product of confession and forgiveness. Many people live their entire lives under a cloud of guilt because they have not learned the secret of release.

Guilt can be a prison into which our mind and spirit are locked for a lifetime. A change of direction for you right here might be the beginning of your dealing with a backup of guilt that is weighing you down and causing your life to be ineffective.

There are three basic negative emotions that can keep us from moving in new directions in our lives: fear, anger, and depression. We have touched lightly upon fear as it relates to this list. Anger and depression are addressed in many good books that are available in bookstores today. If you are struggling with either, I encourage you to do some reading and even seek some professional counseling in your area. All three of these are giant weights that can immobilize your life and keep you from growth changes. They are not easy to deal with because they take years to build up in your life. Sometimes the roots go back to the early years of your life. There are answers for you here if you are willing to look for them.

How to Prepare for a New Direction in Your Life

The thought of doing something brand-new for all of us is highly appealing. It adds sparkle, interest, motivation, and expectancy to our lives. It gives us something to plan for and look forward to. On dark days it gives us a little sunlight to focus upon. New directions take preparation. They seldom happen by some kind of cosmic dust falling upon you at the end of your day. Throughout the pages of the Bible, God was constantly calling people to new directions. Some were immediately willing to answer the call and went forward with an expectant spirit. Others were more reluctant and needed a divine push. Still others tried to run from the call and hide. God has no standard format for leading you and me in new directions. The Scriptures set forth many preliminary things that need to be operative in our daily lives if we are to be led into new areas.

In the chapter on people, we took a quick look at a man

whom God used in a special way in the history of Israel.
In 2 Chronicles 20 we find that Israel is surrounded by
opposing armies and stands in danger of being captured and
destroyed. Jehoshaphat is king at the time. The third verse
tells us that Jeshoshaphat was badly shaken by this news,
and asked for help from the Lord. He sounds a little like
you and me when we are faced with struggles beyond our
size. He could have panicked, he could have cried, he could
have yelled, he could have blamed God. After all, these
armies were from nations that God told Israel earlier to pass
by and not destroy. He could have said, "God, what is this,
anyway?" I want you to notice carefully what this wise king
did at a turning point. .

Verse 3 tells us that Jehoshaphat proclaimed a time of fasting, penitence, and intercession. Faced with annihilation,
Jehoshaphat calmly tells the people to do three things: Fast,
repent, and pray. He doesn't tell them to mobilize for battle. He doesn't suggest that they retreat and run for their
lives. In a scene of potential chaos he suggests the quiet
things that prepare the spirit to hear what God has to say.
I wonder what the Israelites thought. In the next verse it
says that they came to plead with the king. I can imagine
that not a few of them thought he had gotten his signals
crossed. They might have wanted a resolution to this problem in ways they had experienced from the past: Kill the
enemy before the enemy kills you!

But Jehoshaphat had learned something in his lifetime
about a quieting of the spirit in times of stress. He had
learned that God's ways are simply not man's ways. He had
learned the principle of waiting for God's timing and God's
directions.

You and I would have better directions in many areas
of our lives if we would put this principle into operation.
When faced with stress, we usually just fray around the
edges and slowly sink into the west. Or we square our
shoulders and try to take care of things *our* way. How much
further ahead would we be if we followed the principle that

the king laid out for his followers?

Let's look at the three things that Jehoshaphat laid down. The first deals with fasting. Sounds simple, doesn't it? When faced with conflict, challenge, crisis, or change of direction...don't eat! We mentioned earlier that our society seems focused on food. Israel was no different. There are times when that focus needs to be changed. Fasting in and of itself is no magic formula. It was used many times in Scripture as a way of centering on God. Writing in *Celebration of Discipline*, Richard Foster says, "Fasting helps keep our balance in life. How easily we begin to allow nonessentials to take precedence in our lives. How easily we crave things we do not need until we are enslaved by them. Our human cravings and desires are like a river that tends to overflow its banks; fasting helps keep them in their proper channel."

Numerous people have written on the many other values of fasting, such as increased effectiveness in intercessory prayer, guidance in decision-making, increased concentration, deliverance for those in bondage, physical well-being, etc. In this, as in all matters, we can expect God to reward those who diligently seek Him. Fasting demands something from us and opens us up to receiving something from God.

The second admonition from Jehoshaphat was to repent or be in penitence. Penitence means being sorry for having sinned or done wrong. It is an attitude of spirit that is followed by a desire to change one's way. In other words, the king wanted all the people to look at their relationship with God, and if it needed realigning due to sin, they were to take care of it.

We have never lost our need for repentance. We frame it today in different words. Many churches have a Sunday morning prayer of confession that all the people say together. It is the people of God seeking God's forgiveness for their sins and beginning again. Things that we do knowingly or unknowingly block our relationship with God, even as we can cause a barrier to be erected in human relationships. Our job is to be sure that the barriers are removed and the channels are clear in both divine areas and human areas.

The third concern involved intercession before the Lord. The word "intercede" means "to go between." Israel's prayer was that God would intercede between them and the problem and find an answer for them. The process of intercession takes time, whether human or divine in nature. Israel was to show their spirit of united pleading before God as a body. They were one together in their fear as well as their lives.

These were three very simple instructions for Israel: Fast, repent, and pray. As you come to turning points in your life and seek new directions from God, how would these three things apply to you? Are they as valid today as they were in the Old Testament? We know that the end result of this biblical account was that God gave a great victory into the hands of Israel. Jahaziel became God's person to reveal the battle plans. Jehoshaphat called the people of God to the place of readiness to receive the plans.

In the spiritual realm, there is a fourth way that God enables us to move in new directions and to know what those directions are. Since it is more to be experienced than it is something simple to do, many misunderstand it. In Acts 8:26-40 the story is told of Philip's encounter with the Ethiopian eunuch. The Scriptures tell us that "an angel of the Lord spoke to Philip" (v. 26) and that "the Spirit [of the Lord] said to Philip" (v. 29). The indication here is that a personal communication that no one else heard took place between Philip and the angel and the Spirit. Both gave specific directions as to what Philip should do, and Philip followed those directions with outstanding results.

You and I look at this and either say "How?" or else "It was a miracle and it isn't done this way anymore." We think how easy it would be for us to operate like this example: God speaks to us, we respond, and results follow. The truth is that God still speaks but we often do not hear the directions, sometimes due to noise and sometimes due to disbelief. We have all but tuned out God from speaking to us in the ways He spoke to those in the forming of the early church.

I believe that God gives us as clear a set of directions for the things we face today as He did in biblical times. I cannot explain the "how." From my own life and the lives of others, I know He does. The question I want to ask you again is, "Are you listening?"

The early Christians lived with a sense of expectancy and awareness to the operative power of God that we seek to recapture today. They lived with the unexplained and unexplainable. Our modern orientation teaches us that we have to be able to explain how everything is done, even the things that God does. If we can't, then it must not be godly. We have much to learn in this area. Even back in the Old Testament account that we related, when Israel was finally ready to hear the Lord, the Scripture says, "The Spirit of the Lord came upon Jahaziel." We don't need to know the how, why, when, and what for; we only need to know that this is how God sometimes operates. At other times it happens in more simplistic and nonmiraculous ways.

God calls us to turning points that involve a change in direction. He wants us to follow Him into new things in our lives. I can't tell you what that means for you. I only struggle to find out what it means for me. It is easy to be a settler and to live your life as though your only road is the road behind you. I cannot tell you where your turning points are. I can only encourage you to look closely at your journey and ask God for the wisdom to spot them and deal with them when they come your way.

Many years ago I sat by a campfire with a group of young guys at a weekend campout. At the concluding campfire that Sunday night, an invitation was given for us to dedicate our lives to the Lord and follow Him wherever He would lead us. With all the enthusiasm that my 12 years could muster up, I raised my hand indicating that I wanted to follow God's direction for my life. Thirty-nine years later I can tell you where that decision led me: It was a turning point in my life—not a very big one by my standards at that time, but a very real one with future implications in my life. I have had a mountain of turning points since then. Some have been course corrections, others have been charting totally new courses. Some days I felt I was being led through one of those mazes they used to put at the back of comic books. You were supposed to take a pencil and find your way out in one continuous line. You knew there was a way out, if only you could find it. Someone has said, "When all else fails, follow directions." I'm not sure this is the best advice. My version reads, "Before anything fails, follow directions." I pray that you will read your directions at the turning points of your life.

13

God At My Turning Point: Confrontation

13

God At My Turning Point: Confrontation

Are you a confrontive person? Do you walk boldly into a store when you have to return a defective product? When someone has taken advantage of you, do you find it easy to speak directly to that person about the situation? Are you easily intimidated by situations that put you on the defensive?

If you are a part of the real world, you are probably nodding a silent *yes* along with me. I struggle with confrontive situations. I have tried to explore my reasons and have come up with a few. First, I really don't enjoy any situation that puts me in conflict with anyone else. Second, I don't always know what to say in a conflict. Third, I am afraid I will lose the confrontation and look bad in other people's opinion and in my own. Fourth, I am afraid of what the end result will be.

If you grew up in a home where confrontation was the order of the day, you will probably join the 20 percent of our society who welcome it and handle it very well. I once read a book called *Power Plays*, in which the author simply set forth the many ways a person can get the upper hand in any and all situations. Step by step you were told how to handle and win any confrontive situation with another

human being. That book was similar to a bestseller a number of years ago called *Winning Through Intimidation*. Similar principles were shared that would put you one up on
any other person. The ultimate goal in both books was to
put you in the place of power and control.

I confess that some things I read in these books were helpful. Others made me shudder because I could never fit the
mold of living out the intimidative role with other people.
Even feeling that, I have had different people tell me that
I intimidated them. That makes me wonder, because I don't
see myself that way, nor do I want to be that way. But I
am aware that anyone in any form of leadership can be
somewhat intimidating and confrontive to those in a lesser
position. Every one of us is a leader to someone, even if it
is just the family dog or cat. The meekest clerk at the Depart-
ment of Motor Vehicles can intimidate me when I go to
renew my driver's license. The reason? He or she is in control of my destiny at that point, and I am not. I feel the same
way when I go to my doctor or dentist or auto mechanic.
Since I know very little in those areas, I am not in control
and am mildly intimidated. If they do something wrong, I
have an even harder time going back to them to confront
the issue.

According to Webster, the word "confront" means "to
face; stand or meet face to face." It also means "to face or
oppose boldly, defiantly, or antagonistically." Just letting that
ring in our ears would send most of us running in the opposite direction. Yet you and I cannot live and grow without
confronting things in our life. Many of us fall into the trap
of putting it off into the future somewhere. The problem
with this is that we increase our fear of confrontation and
build the problem into a mountain-size obstacle. I remember once receiving a letter on a Friday from the Internal Rev-
enue Service. It was official and was addressed to me with
a typewriter and not a mailing-machine label. I knew it was
important, and I feared its contents. I knew I must have
goofed somewhere in my tax-filing history, and I was going

to be confronted with a very real problem. I decided not to open the letter until Monday morning so that the contents would not spoil my weekend. Guess what? My weekend was spoiled worrying about the contents. On Monday I opened it, only to find that I had made a tax-filing mistake . . . in my favor! I was notified that I would be receiving a check for a small amount of money within 60 days. Was I ever relieved! And was I ever sorry that I had not opened the letter immediately!

Confronting people, problems, life situations, and even ourselves is a daily part of life's agenda. The only way I know to avoid this is to live in a cave in the desert and become a hermit. Then the only person you will have to deal with is yourself. Since most of us cannot afford that kind of solitary exile, we have to choose to deal with confrontation in the best way we can. An excellent book that speaks on this issue is David Augsburger's *Caring Enough to Confront*. It addresses many sides of confrontation that we will not go into here. It is practical and wise, and I highly recommend it to you.

We *do* want to look at the biblical side of how we are confronted by God to bring us and take us through turning points in our lives. There are some very strong issues with which God confronts you and me as we grow. The four we want to look at form a strong foundation for our growth.

In the Scriptures, God confronted people to whom He wanted to give directions in three different ways. He sometimes spoke verbally to that person, either in a voice heard by all or in a voice heard only by the person addressed. Both Moses and Saul fall into this category. Sometimes God spoke through other people, using them as messengers to deliver His directives. A third method that God employed came in the form of life situations. God used the familiar and the everyday to speak to people. A great portion of the Gospels portrays this style of direction and communication.

The Confrontation of Love

Jesus lived out a daily confrontation of love in the three years of His public ministry. He continually called people to the life of love. When He spent those hours with the disciples on the Mount of Olives preparing them for His leaving, the essence of His message was centered in love. He put His own love on the line as an example by telling them to love each other just as He loved them. What He had carefully modeled He now called into execution in the lives of those closest to Him. There were a million other things He could have called their attention to, but He focused on love.

When Jesus healed people of their sicknesses, His acts of compassion carried the personal message "I LOVE YOU!" He was sowing the seeds of love in a way that was believable. You and I always know when we are really loved. It can be expressed in a verbal way, but many times it comes packaged in the nonverbal. With it comes a surrounding feeling of warmth and caring. We know only one thing: When it's there, we don't want it to disappear. When we experience a little of it, we desire a whole lot more. We all develop an insatiable appetite for the expression of love.

Jesus' acts of healing were in effect confrontations of love. There are over 40 recorded instances of healings in Jesus' public ministry. Sometimes to one person and sometimes to many people who were healed, Jesus confronted the hurts and heartaches of life with the healing power of love.

A pointed confrontation in loving occurred when a Pharisee named Nicodemus sought out Jesus under the cover of darkness. Nicodemus came to recognize and affirm Jesus—who He was and what He did. He perhaps came with other questions and thoughts that somehow never got verbalized. Jesus quickly used the encounter to center in on spiritual rebirth and its implications. He explained divine intentions to Nicodemus in the words, "For God so loved the world that He gave His only begotten Son, that whoever believes in Him should not perish but have everlasting life" (John

3:16). Jesus clarified to Nicodemus what love does, what love is, and what love will always be.

One of Jesus' most direct confrontations in loving came in John chapter 21. In His third appearance to the disciples after the resurrection, He confronted Peter with the words "Simon, son of John, do you love me more than these?" Peter responded affirmatively, and Jesus asked the question twice more. Again Peter responded with a yes. Jesus was not seeking a personal affirmation of Peter's love for Him so that He could knowingly walk away smiling and saying to Himself, "Peter really loves me, and that feels good." He questioned Peter so that Peter could respond and receive the challenge of transmitting that love to others. Three times Jesus echoed the challenge of love when He said, "Feed My lambs...tend My sheep...feed My sheep." Jesus was in effect saying to Peter, "If you love Me, you will share that love by caring for those I care for."

Jesus put Himself in the place of being the conduit of love between Peter and people everywhere. Peter was confronted with love as it transmits to pastoral care in people's lives. From His directive to the disciples on the Mount of Olives to love one another, Jesus now moved love into a larger framework. Love must first and always be personal before it can be general. It must be specific before it can be collective.

Jesus confronted people with God's love, His own love, the love of each other, and the love of everyone. You and I are confronted with love in that same way. A turning point in loving is deciding to become a lover. It does not come easily, and it doesn't happen overnight. It takes time and flourishes best when practiced most.

How are you doing in carrying out your confrontations of love? Who in your life and community needs to be touched by your love? Who needs to be tended, shepherded, fed?

The Confrontation of Honesty

Have you ever struggled with honesty in your life? This

is not intended to mean that you are dishonest and fight to attain some dimension of honesty. I believe that most people are basically honest but struggle with just how honest they really should be in some situations.

You have just finished a wonderful dinner that someone else has cooked for you—only it wasn't so wonderful. She served several dishes that were not among your favorites. At the conclusion of the dessert, you push your chair back and exclaim to your hostess, "That was a wonderful dinner, Marge! You served all my favorites!" Were you really being honest? Should you, could you, have said what you really felt? This is a tough decision, to be sure, but inside your own spirit you knew you were not honest.

You are probably thinking that my illustration is such a small one in life compared to the major issues of honesty. And you are right—it is small. But the question that most of us wrestle with is where to draw the line in honesty. Should we be totally honest in big things and semihonest in little things? Honest if it doesn't hurt anyone and dishonest if it does? Scripture tells us to speak the truth in love, but we struggle with what that really means and how the implications of doing it will affect our lives.

Every day we are confronted with turning points in honesty. Every day we promise we will be more direct and honest to those around us, but then we slip back into the fog of semitruth in order not to hurt ourselves or someone else.

We are called to live honestly and in honesty. It is a process that we sweat and struggle with every day. As we grow in spiritual maturity, our levels of honesty rise. As we learn to love, we learn to love honestly.

We can learn much from Jesus' style of living and practicing honesty. He could confront people in honesty, and they received it from Him. The only ones who fought His honesty were the ruling authorities and the religious hierarchy. When He told the truth about the Pharisees as religious rulers and called them whited sepulchres, they sought to kill Him. They did not say, "Yes, Jesus, You are right, and we will start to change now."

When He cleared the temple of religious profiteers, they were not transformed by His honesty. They began to plot against Him. A lesson in honesty tells us that honesty does not always bring about the results we desire. When you follow rightful convictions, you don't always win applause.

When Jesus talked with the woman at the well and finally told her she had been married numerous times and even now was living with a man who was not her husband, she did not run from Him but asked permission to bring her household to Him for further guidance. She marveled at His honesty but was not turned off by it. Rather, honesty drew her to Jesus.

In a bold discussion with the disciples in John chapter 6, Jesus said, "There are some of you who do not believe." As a result of Jesus' bold and honest statement here, some of the disciples withdrew from Him and ceased to follow Him. He could have said, "I know some of you are having problems right now, but hang tough and things will work out." He simply called the situation in honesty, and some could not accept His honesty. They were repelled, in contrast to the Samaritan woman, who was attracted. Honesty does both, and its results are unpredictable.

In Acts chapter 5 we have a later account of the results of dishonesty in the lives of Ananias and Sapphira. They both lied about a sales transaction and were quickly struck dead—a tough lesson to learn about honesty for the early church! I doubt that anyone who had been close by or heard about it later would have a problem with their own personal honesty!

Jesus raised the standard of honesty in His own ministry. It remains there for you and me to struggle with and grow in. Honesty and our freedom to employ it in our lives can be a great turning point.

The Confrontation of Truth

The confrontation of truth is a vital part of the confrontation in honesty. You cannot have one without the other. We battle today to find out what is true in all areas of our lives. We hear things being said and try to find out if they are true. We hear a rumor and want to know if it is more than hearsay. People swear to tell the whole truth and nothing but the truth and then proceed to pile lie upon lie. We read newspaper commentaries on the lives of other people and wonder how much of it is true and how much is fiction or a figment of someone's imagination. We hear so much about so many people that we wonder how much of it is true. Some days we believe everything we hear while other days we want to believe nothing. We seem to be traveling further and further down a road that distorts truth with increasing frequency. Because we have become an information society, we increasingly question whether that information is true.

Jesus sought to draw people to the truth of God in His ministry. One day, talking to a group of Jews who were believers, He told them, "You shall know the truth, and the truth shall make you free." Jesus raised a standard for truth that became a hallmark for His earthly ministry. His words have been carried into the mainstream of society for centuries to attest that truth is and always will be freeing. Even though in John's Gospel He was speaking to the Jews about the real truth of God as opposed to their truth as they knew it, His words still electrify those who live with oppression and nontruth around our planet.

We have all had the experience of being caught in a lie at one time in our lives. The tendency is to add to the lie and make it larger rather than to tell the truth. Lies can hide other lies, but only truth can dissolve them and set us free. We have experienced the new freedom and relief that comes when we own up to dishonesty and untruth. Professional counselors have long learned the value of getting their clients to deal with truth. Healing can come only in a truthful setting. It releases us from the need to be hiding where we have been untruthful.

Living in truth is living in the place of freedom. We confront it, we choose it, and we begin living it a day at a time. We let truth invade the small areas of our lives as well as the big ones. We speak truth, we think truth, and we live truth. When Paul wrote a letter to the Philippian Christians, he said, "Finally, brethren, whatever things are *true*, whatever things are noble, whatever things are just, whatever things are pure, whatever things are lovely, whatever things are of good report, if there is any virtue and if there is anything praiseworthy—*meditate* on these things" (Philippians 4:8). Good thought! It tells us that these things are to be dealt with in our minds before we practice them in our lives.

The Confrontation of Change

Have you ever thought of yourself as a catalyst for change in the lives of those around you? Do you see yourself helping others to reach out and embrace needed changes in their lives? We can be both an agent for change and subject to change in our lives. Healthy living includes both.

Change, as we stated earlier, is both scary and exciting. We often do not enter into change points unless we are dramatically confronted by them. Jesus told people that He had come to bring them life, life more abundantly. He could also have said that He came to bring change, change more abundantly. Life doesn't scare people quite as much as change does. For Jesus, though, to have life meant that you had to be willing to change. As He moved through the lives of people in the Gospels, we discover that He seldom left people without some new changes being introduced to their lives. Some welcomed what He brought while others were frightened by it.

One of our greatest fears in confronting change is that we will change not for the better but the worse. If things around us change, it will be not for the better but the worse. That's why it is often easier to leave things as they are than to walk carefully out on the seas of change.

Change starts with desire, the small spark that starts burning within us and slowly consumes our uncertainties. Desire is followed by pursuit and implementation of change. As change grows in our lives, we see the fresh results and we begin to welcome it rather than fear it.

Jesus confronted people with the question of change. He seldom said, "How would you like to change your entire life?" Instead, He asked people how they would like to *begin* changing their lives. To the woman caught in adultery, He became her change agent. He freed her from her lifestyle, and that was a major change. He freed her from man's judgment, and another major change occurred. He introduced her to a new life with the words "Neither do I condemn you; go and sin no more" (John 8:11). He confronted her with the process of change and guided her a step at a time into it. Change is not a hammer that you hit people over the head with. It is a road map that you guide people upon. Jesus knew how to do that in a gentle yet honest spirit. In His presence, changes began because of His gentle confrontation of life-changing issues.

We want to change, but we want it done overnight. We want those around us to change, but we want it done in two overnights. We want God to confront us with His changes, but we want it yesterday.

God can and will bring you to the place of change in your life if you will ask Him. He will not give you a complete guide to what and how He will make those changes. He will reveal His plan for you just a step at a time. And some days it will look like a rocky road while other days you will be glad you asked, and will start out.

God is at any and all turning points in your life. He is confronting you with love, honesty, truth, and change. The response is up to you. You can remain as you are, or you can claim your turning point.

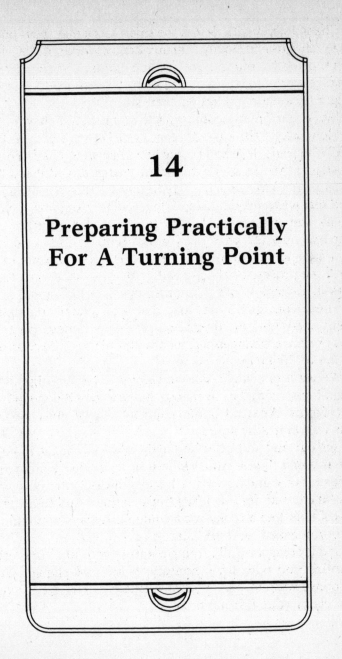

14

Preparing Practically
For A Turning Point

14

Preparing Practically
For A Turning Point

A number of years ago our family lived in Florida only a few miles from the beautiful white-sand beaches. Our children were small at the time, and their idea of a fun day was to pack up and head for the beach. Their comment was, "Let's go to the beach!" They jumped into the car and yelled back at us to hurry and asked why we were taking so long. The reason we were taking so long was that we were trying to pack the contents of our entire house into the trunk of our car to take to the beach. You don't just *go* to the beach—you attack it prepared for anything that can happen to you while there. It wasn't so bad going, but coming home was a different story. It took hours to wash that wonderfully fine Florida sand out of everything we owned.

At the end of our nine-hour orgy of family fun, our children always told us what fun we had, and asked when we could go again. The truth is that they had fun and we had all the preparation and cleanup. Having fun takes preparation. Living life takes preparation. Navigating your turning points takes preparation. Too many of us are not willing to do the things that equip us to handle our turning points. We end up like the man who shot at nothing and hit it!

How do you practically prepare to face a turning point in your life? Is it like going to the beach, going camping, or heading out on a 3000-mile vacation by car? I believe it is all of the above and a whole lot more. I have learned some things about my own turning points that I want to share with you.

A long time ago I read somewhere that there are four basic stages that we go through in preparing for any major change in our life. If we face our changes in a logical pattern, we will experience each of these. They are preparation, incubation, illumination, and actualization. Let's look at each of them and see how they fit our lives.

Preparation

I believe you can collide head-on with some turning points in your life with little or no time for preparation. They are just suddenly there in front of you, and you must act on them. But for most of us, that kind of experience would fall into the 20-percent-or-less category. Most of our turning points are of the "slow-buildup" variety. This kind of turning point gives us preparation time.

Practical preparation means first of all doing your homework. Homework is an ugly word to most of us. When our academic years finally ended, we happily put our homework to rest. Someone should have told us that we will have to do homework until we die! Homework is research, and research is digging for all the information we need that will help us navigate a turning point. If our turning point is a move to a new area of the country, we need to read everything we can about that area. We need to subscribe to its local newspapers so that we can read about the day-to-day news of that area. We need to talk with people who have lived there or are living there. We need to go there and look around, talk to people, ask questions, and breathe the life of that community, state, or place.

Most of us fear what remains a mystery to us. Once a form

of familiarity sets in, fear dissolves. Homework is filling the pages of notebooks with facts. Can I suggest a bottom-line practicality here? When you start facing or thinking about a turning point in your life, buy a spiral notebook and start filling it with your questions, your answers, your observations, your likes, your dislikes, your fears, your excitement. Don't leave anything out, as this is your personal journal for your turning point. When you have completed your journey, you will have a road map that you designed. You will be amazed what this will do for you when you face other turning points in your journey.

If you are thinking about a career change, do the same thing. Buy a notebook and start your turning-point file. Decide to do your homework. Homework will never be fun, but it will take the fright out of what you face as you become more acquainted with it. No matter what your planned, projected, or right-now turning point is, go at it with a plan. Don't be afraid to ask questions, but don't always absorb the answers as final truth. Remember, in most instances people give their *own* opinion. It is good for input and comparison, but you need not accept it as an ultimate answer for your own life.

Another practical suggestion is to also start keeping a ''dreaming of a turning point'' notebook. As I have moved deeper into the challenge of writing, I have started keeping a notebook in this area. I scribble ideas, thoughts, concepts, and dreams into it all the time. Some will become a reality, some not. But if I write them down, I will not lose them.

Practical preparation also means talking things through with trusted friends. Your best friends should know you better than other people do. If they have a history with you, they will be able to creatively brainstorm ideas with you. Brainstorming, being creative, is not a solitary pursuit. We hitchhike on the thoughts of other people.

Businesses are turning more and more to employee-brainstorming sessions today when they run into problems or seek to outline long-range growth and planning. I believe that great ideas stem from the catalyst of thoughts shared by a group of people who know and trust each other. I admit that most of us don't have a lot of people who fit that category, but we all have a few. Good and trusted friends want to see you grow and reach your potential. They will not become envious or jealous if you are successful and they helped you along on your journey. I don't believe that you simply ask your friends what they think you should do in any situation; you ask them to *explore a situation* with you and give you objective input to think about. This process takes time; it is not done over lunch if you are facing some major turning point in your life.

A third practical suggestion deals with the spiritual component of prayer. I am not sure it should be placed third in some list; it might well be the first thing you should consider if your desire is to serve the Lord in all areas of your life. But I want to caution you not to just pray and then do nothing. In the Scriptures, prayer is followed by action. Prayer prepares us for what is to follow, but we must never forget that God also gave us a mind to use and a sound thinking process to employ. Ideas of change are planted in our spirit by the Lord and are also sent to us through other people. This is less mystical and more practical than most of us are willing to believe. A job counselor told me the other day that most jobs were found not by advertising or employment agencies but through a network of friends and acquaintances. I believe that many of our turning points also come about by a similar process. Each of us comes equipped with a surrounding network of people in life. If we are open, God can use those people to bring fresh new ideas and challenges into our lives. Perhaps a starting prayer would be "Lord, send some people for my projected turning point." It may take time for the people to be placed in your life, so don't try to hurry the process. God is in the business of using people. We need to prayerfully be in the business of allowing God to use them in our lives.

Homework, research, networking, brainstorming, praying

—these are the practical things of preparation. Saturation and study in these areas will equip us with confidence to face a turning point. Lack of these things will send us scurrying about in confusion and disarray.

Incubation

Incubation is a waiting process. Most of us are not equipped to be good waiters. Our world is designed on the human side to be a "right now" kind of existence. Everything is designed to help us save time rather than process time. From business to leisure, the credo is to do it faster and smarter. I am not sure what we are to do with the leftover time that is supposedly being added to our lives. Nature still reminds us that God works in a time process. Planting and harvest are the result of a patient Creator. Do you ever think that God is still trying to tell us something by surrounding us daily with His way of getting things done?

I have learned a few things about the process of incubation in my own life. First, I get an idea. It may come from anywhere. Then I process that idea within my own mind: Think about it, pray about it, start gathering information on it. I talk with my friends about it. I seek to do all the things I mentioned in the past page or two. Then I cool it! I put it on a shelf and do nothing with it for a period of time. I let it simmer and stew and brew in my nonconscious mind. It's in the file drawer and out of sight. I give it a chance to grow and form and make sense. I don't fully understand how this process really works, but for me (and hopefully for you) it does. Then, when I open the file drawer at the proper time, the concept, idea, thought, turning point is ready to be put into gear. Some call this a period of gestation, whose secondary meaning is "a plan of the mind." I write using basically this process. I have four new book ideas now simmering away in the files of my mind. They may or may not ever happen, but they are quietly going through the incubation process.

Too many of us, in our impatience, spoil great ideas for change in our life by trying to "push the river." We need to learn the principle of "going with the flow," much as God uses in nature. We want to speed the process of going from seed to feed in 12 hours. Someone has wisely said, "If you want to grow mushrooms, you can do it overnight, but if you want to grow an oak, it takes a thousand years."

Give God the time to do His work while your ideas are cooking in your mind and spirit. He is never in a hurry and will properly prepare the things around your idea that may lead to a turning point.

Illumination

Have you ever been caught in a personal struggle when, no matter which way you turned, there seemed to be no answer? Have you ever gone through the preparation and incubation stages of an idea or a turning point only to come up against a brick wall or a blind alley? Correct processes don't always guarantee sudden insights or dynamic answers. Illumination is insight that we previously have not had. It can come in a sudden flash for no explainable reason. It can hit you at three in the morning or three in the afternoon. It can come through comments or suggestions from other people. It can be profound or it can be simple. When it happens, you wonder how you could have labored so long in the dark. Illumination is the revelation of possibilities that can bring sunlight into your spirit. It is the "Aha!" or "Eureka!" that comes at different times to all of us. If there is a mystical aspect to opening the doors to turning points, illumination or insight is it. A believer in God's power in lives would say that it is the place where God breaks through to each of us and gives us the insight we have sought from Him. It would and could be an answer to our prayers revealed in a way that defies explanation.

Actualization

Actualizing is the *do it* in our four practical processes. It is that point in time when we have done all the other things and have reached a decision. As I travel around, I meet aspiring writers who tell me they are going to write a book someday. Some of them have great stories to tell and would love to tell them. But most of these stories will never be told except in the corridors of the mind of the prospective author. The reason: He or she never sits down at the typewriter, blocks out the time, and begins to write. Books written in the mind will never be inscribed on the lives of those around us. To do is to work, and work is still an inglorious labor that most of us seek to avoid.

To do is a pole-vaulter running down a runway at a track meet and inserting the pole in the groove in the turf and beginning his journey toward the crossbar. *To do* is running a 26-mile marathon. *To do* is beginning a march of faith, much as Joshua did around the walls of Jericho. *To do* is acting on your preparation and trusting that the process will take you through your turning point. *To do* is resolving to not turn back. Paul said something wise about this in Philippians 3:13,14: "Brethren, I do not count myself to have apprehended; but one thing I do: forgetting those things which are behind and reaching forward to those things which are ahead, I press toward the goal for the prize of the upward call of God in Christ Jesus." Paul knew the value of the *to do*. He committed to what was ahead, not what was behind. He reached out to the future, which for him was the call of God in his life.

You can do all the homework and preparation you want to, but if it eventually doesn't lead to commitment to action, you have wasted your time. Many people get so bogged down in preparation that actualization never happens. Other people do a lot of talking but never commit to the action.

Turning points must be action points if they are to help us grow! Living with them for me means several things.

First, it means that I open my life wide to possible changes. I don't live with an arms-folded approach to life. I live with my arms wide open to life stance. I learn to embrace the opportunities and possibilities that come my way. I become an adventurer and explorer rather than a settler. I welcome the new and the "not so sure" into my life. I live with the prayer "Lord, change me!"

Second, I open my life up to the "no-guarantee" way of living. This means that I am not afraid of making a wrong decision or going in a wrong direction. I know I have the freedom to fail and begin again. I learn that there are no guarantees outside of the guarantee of God's love and His promise that He will be with me in every decision and wherever I go.

Third, I become a risk-taker. We have already spoken about the implications of this. I just want to line it up for you on the shopping list.

Fourth, I realize that one turning point connects me to another one. If I miss the one I need to make, I may well miss others that offer good direction to my life. As I missed a turnoff the other day on one of our freeways I thought, "No problem—I'll take the next one and double back." But the next one was closed, and the next one after that was the wrong way. After about 20 turns and several miles, I was able to get back to where I wanted to be. I was sorry I had missed the turning point!

Fifth, I expand my belief to include the fact that God is always in charge of my turning points. He doesn't send me there alone. He walks with me through them one step at a time.

Finally, living with turning points will be exciting and scary for me. Avoiding them will be stunting to my life and growth.